T0086258

Isaiah 26:3—4
"PERFECT PEACE XIII"
1 Kings 19:1—18

VANESSA RAYNER

authorHOUSE®

AuthorHouse™
1663 Liberty Drive
Bloomington, IN 47403
www.authorhouse.com
Phone: 1 (800) 839-8640

Published by AuthorHouse 12/18/2017

ISBN: 978-1-5462-1957-6 (sc)
ISBN: 978-1-5462-1956-9 (e)

Library of Congress Control Number: 2016905764

Print information available on the last page.

A GIFT . . .

Presented to

_____

From

_____

Date

_____

ANSWER FEAR WITH FAITH;
NOTHING ELSE IS EFFECTIVE
AGAINST IT!

TABLE OF CONTENTS

Theme

The message of **Isaiah 26:3-4** is "Perfect Peace." This is the distinct and unifying composition of this book with the subtitle *1 Kings 19:1-18*.

A Song of Praise

You will keep in perfect peace all who trust in you,
all whose thoughts are fixed on you!
Trust in the Lord always,
for the Lord God is the eternal Rock.
Isaiah 26:3-4 NLT

PS: Isaiah 26 has 21 verses.

PRAYER

Oh, Heavenly Father,
I thank you for another day, and another
opportunity to write another book.
I pray that your people are prospering
daily in their spirit, soul, and body
by reading, Perfect Peace Books.

Oh, Heavenly Father,
I ask in Jesus' name that the Holy Spirit will
help readers to remember Your word.
I pray it will give them peace, and joy,
at a time they need it the most.
I thank You for blessing those that help
make Your work able to go forth.

Oh, Heavenly Father,
You have made it clear that You will
reward those that bless your servant.
It could be through prayer, words of encouragement,
to giving that person a cup of water.

Oh, Heavenly Father,
I give you all the Glory, Honor
and Praise in Jesus' name.

Amen.

Author's Notes

Author notes generally provide a way to add extra information to one's book that may be awkward and inappropriate to include in the text of the book itself. It provides supplemental contextual details on the aspects of the book. It can help readers understand the book content and the background details of the book better. The times and dates of researching, reading, and gathering this information are not included; mostly when I typed on it.

2020; Sunday, 16 July 2017; Started working on this book, adding small details and thoughts.

1921; Friday, 28 July 2017

2033; Saturday, 29 July 2017

0550; Sunday, 30 July 2017

2129; Monday, 31 July 2017

1800; Tuesday, 01 August 2017

1722; Friday, 04 August 2017

0356; Saturday, 05 August 2017

0735; Sunday, 06 August 2017

1548; Monday, 07 August 2017

0610; Tuesday, 08 August 2017; Must share . . . Woke up for work around 0530 with a tune in my head, "Darling, If you want me to, I would die for you," and I could hear the music playing in the background which sounds like Princes. I said, Father God what's going on, as hard as I worked on this book last night. I just smiled to myself and headed to the kitchen, as I enter the hallway, I heard Father God in a gentle whisper say, "I'm singing that to you." Glory Hallelujah!

1631; Wednesday, 09 August 2017

0824; Sunday, 13 August 2017

1421; Monday, 14 August 2017; Left work with severe muscle spasms to go to the doctor's office. Doctor F. Everson took me off work until Monday the 21st because of pain, and the meds I will be taking. I'm going to work on this book until I fall asleep. Hallelujah, Anyhow!

0922; Tuesday, 15 August 2017; Feeling much better. Lord, I Praise Your Holy Name! I don't understand everything, but I trust you in everything. Sah-tas-me-o-so! Hallelujah! Thank You, Jesus . . . Thank You, Jesus . . .

0612; Wednesday, 16 August 2017

0726; Thursday, 17 August 2017

2105; Friday, 18 August 2017

1615; Monday, 21 August 2017

1855; Tuesday, 22 August 2017

1530; Wednesday, 23 August 2017

1954; Thursday, 24 August 2017

2107; Friday, 25 August 2017

0000; Saturday, 26 August 2017

0744; Sunday, 27 August 2017

1550; Monday, 28 August 2017

1551; Wednesday, 30 August 2017

1551; Thursday, 31 August 2017

1943; Friday, 01 September 2017

0418; Saturday, 02 September 2017

0753; Sunday, 03 September 2017

0342; Monday, 04 September 2017; Happy Labor Day.

1550; Tuesday, 05 September 2017

1534; Wednesday, 06 September 2017; Happy Birthday Dad! ~ Rev. Ambous Lee Moore ~ 93 years old ~ RIP

1827; Thursday, 07 September 2017

2200; Friday, 08 September 2017

0940; Saturday, 09 September 2017

0703; Sunday, 10 September 2017

1540; Monday, 11 September 2017

1628; Wednesday, 13 September 2017; Happy B'day ~ Son, Charles A. Jones Jr.

1521; Friday, 15 September 2017

0111; Saturday, 16 September 2017

0724; Sunday, September 17, 2017; Happy Birthday ~ Great Niece, Raven Kelley

1537; Monday, 18 September 2017

1648; Tuesday, 19 September 2017

1550; Wednesday, 20 September 2017; Just finished talking with Apostle Dorothy Smith, the conversation really encouraged my soul. Lord, I thank you for her.

1516; Thursday, 21 September 2017

2000; Friday, 22 September 2017

0611; Sunday, 24 September

0754; Sunday, 24 September 2017; Just dropped in my spirit, to add two short informative chapters; 14 & 15. Hallelujah!

2150; Tuesday, 26 September 2017

1544; Wednesday, 27 September 2017

0700; Sunday, 01 October 2017

1558; Tuesday, 03 October 2017

1915; Wednesday, 04 October 2017

1629; Thursday, 05 October 2017

1644; Friday, 06 October 2017

1932; Saturday, 07 October 2017; I attended the "Wilt Thou Be Made Whole?" Fall Conference in Sikeston, MO. It was hosted by Apostle, Dr. Dorothy J. Smith at Pastor/Apostle Betty Ware's church named Powerhouse of God. The message was given by Apostle, Dr. Brenda Bush from West Memphis, Arkansas. I was truly blessed! Praise God.

0708; Sunday, 08 October 2017

1523; Tuesday, 10 October 2017

1539; Wednesday, 11 October 2017

2045; Thursday, 12 October 2017

0651; Saturday, 14 October 2017

0638; Sunday, 15 October 2017

1630; Monday, 16 October 2017

1849; Thursday, 19 October 2017; A lot has happened since Monday's evening, but Father God is my everything!

1747; Friday, 20 October 2017

0603; Saturday, 21 October 2017

1833; Sunday, 22 October 2017; Woke up this morning about 0646 with the word "Expectation" on my mind. Last night on the telephone prayer line, Prophet C. L. Allen, who I never met in person, preached on "Expectation." He started from Psalms

62:5, "My soul, wait thou only upon God; for my expectation is from him." The message surrounding "Expectation, God and Us" is still ringing in my soul. Hallelujah!

1713; Tuesday, 24 October 2017

1827; Friday, 27 October 2017

1823; Tuesday, 07 November 2017

0201; Tuesday, 21 November 2017; Uploading Manuscript. Glory Be to God!

Preface

Isaiah 26:3-4, "Perfect Peace XIII" ~ 1st Kings 19:1-18

The book <u>Isaiah 26:3-4, "Perfect Peace XIII" 1st Kings 19:1-18</u> is the 13th book in a series called Isaiah 26:3-4, "Perfect Peace." Glory be to God!

It all started from how I drew near to the LORD in my workplace by keeping my mind on Him. I related numbers, you see throughout the day, everywhere, on almost everything on Him, His word, biblical events, and facts to give me peace in the midst of chaos.

It's our desire for you to discover the power of the Holy Spirit by numbers, words, places, people, and things related to the biblical event that occurred in 1st Kings 19:1-18.

Remember, the LORD Jesus <u>PROMISED us tribulation</u> while we were in this world.

These things, I have spoken unto you,
that in me ye might have peace.
In the world ye shall have tribulation:
But be of good cheer; I have overcome the world.
John 16:33 KJV

However, we have been <u>PROMISED His peace</u> while we endure these trials, tribulations, troubles, and tests. Perfect Peace is given only to those whose mind and heart reclines upon the LORD. God's peace is increased in us according to the knowledge of His Holy Word.

**Grace and peace be multiplied unto you
through the knowledge of God,
and of Jesus our LORD.**
2 Peter 1:2 KJV

THANKS   *To the Readers . . .*

As a disciple of the LORD Jesus Christ, I have learned true success comes when we are seeking and striving to do God's purpose for our lives. Our real happiness lies in doing God's will; not in fame and fortune.

Thank you for your support. Thank you for helping me spread "Perfect Peace" through your e-mail, Facebook, Twitter, LinkedIn, Instagram, Tumblr, Messenger and etc. accounts to your family, friends, neighbors, co-workers, church family, internet social friends, and associates.

Remember, you may not know until you get to heaven just how much a song you sung, kind words spoken by you or even a book you suggested reading, at the right moment, encourage a person to keep on going when a few minutes before they were tempted to give up on life and their walk with the LORD.

I greatly appreciate your love and kindness to this ministry.

ACKNOWLEDGEMENTS

First and foremost, I wish to express my sincere gratitude to *"Our Heavenly Father"* for his guidance, patience, and lovingkindness throughout the writing of this book.

INTRODUCTION

For Those Who Want To Be Kept In "Perfect Peace"

This book was prepared and written to open your mind to a "Perfect Peace" that comes only from God. I'm striving to elevate you into a "Unique and Profound" awareness of God's presence around you at all time.

According to some people, it's hard to keep your mind on the LORD. While most Christians will agree that if you keep your mind stayed on the LORD, He will keep you in "Perfect Peace." This is why so many people enjoy going to church on Sundays and attending midweek services for peace and joy that they receive, but only for a short time.

You can experience the peace of the LORD throughout the day and every day. His unspeakable joy, his strength, his "Perfect Peace" in the midst of the storm whether it's at work, home, college, school, etc. You can also experience this peace, even when your day is going well.

This concept of this book was placed in my spirit by our Father, which art in heaven, to help me when he allowed Satan to test me at my workplace until he finished molding me into a MAP; (Minister/Ambassador/Pastor).

Throughout these pages, I will be focussing on biblical events, and facts surrounding 1 Kings 19:1-18. However, I am sure much more can be said on this passage of scriptures, so these subjects serve merely as an introduction and are not exhaustive by any means.

DEDICATION

This book is dedicated to Pastor S. Gaines who preached from 1ˢᵗ Kings 19:1-18, the first time I attended service at Bellevue Baptist Church, Memphis, Tn. The message was titled, "<u>The God Who Whisper</u>."

CHAPTER 1

1st Kings

In the Christian Bible, 1st Kings is the 11th book in the Old Testament and consists of 22 chapters. In the original Hebrew Bible, 1st and 2nd Kings is a single book called the Books of Kings. The Books of Kings is the 4th book of Nevi'im, the 2nd division of the Tanakh, in the sub-group called the Former Prophets. The Tanakh consists of 24 books. In the Septuagint, Samuels and Kings were divided into four books and Kings became books III and IV. Jewish tradition acknowledges Jeremiah the prophet as the author of 1st Kings, although Bible scholars are divided on this issue.

Notes of Interests: The Hebrew Bible or Hebrew Scripture is called Tanakh. The Tanakh is known to Christians as the Old Testament. The Tanakh has three divisions; Torah, Nevi'im, and Ketuvim. Torah means "law." It consists of the five books of Moses. It's called the Pentateuch by its Greek name which means "five scrolls." Nevi'im is another division in the Torah which means "Prophets." The Nevi'im division is divided into two sections; the Earlier Prophets, and the Latter Prophets. The Earlier Prophets are generally historical, while the Latter Prophets contains prophecies. Ketuvim means "Writings." It is divided into three categories which are the Wisdom Books of Job, Ecclesiastes, Proverbs, then the Poetry Books of Psalms, Lamentations, Song of Solomon, and finally, the Historical Books of Ezra-Nehemiah and Chronicles.

~~~

The Books of Kings are the last two books of a series of books referred to as the Deuteronomistic History which was written while the first Temple was standing. First and Second Kings are a continuation of the books of Samuel. It records the events and history of Solomon and the succeeding kings of Judah and Israel. The Southern Kingdom (Judah) had twenty kings, and the Northern Kingdom (Israel) had nineteen kings. They cover a period of 400 years. This history comes from the books of Joshua, Judges, Samuels, and Kings; but not Chronicles.

Notes of Interests:The books of Chronicles are believed by some scholars were written to provide an explanation for the destruction of the Kingdom of Judah by Babylon in 586 BC and the return of the people from exile. When Cyrus of Persia conquered Babylonia in 539 BC, about one year later he gave the Jewish people permission to return back to their homeland. The books of Ezra and Nehemiah in the Old Testament tell about this biblical event. The books from the prophets Haggai and Zechariah are written from this era.

~~~

The two Books of Kings present a history of ancient Israel and Judah, beginning with King David and ends with the king of Babylon, 960-560 BC. Kings open with the building of the Temple and end with the burning of the Temple. Kings open with David's first's successor to the throne of his kingdom, Solomon, and ends with David's last successor, Jehoiachin, released from captivity by the king of Babylon.

The themes in 1st Kings is idolatry has disastrous consequences. It shows how idolatry brought down the wisest man in the world, King Solomon. It brought destruction to both individuals and nations. Idolatry is the worship of an idol, physical image or created object that is considered a god. First Kings records the rise and fall of King Solomon, his involvement with false gods, and pagan customs of his foreign wives. It also describes the decline of Israel when they turned away from Jehovah, the One True God.

The 8 major false gods of the Old Testaments are listed below:

Ashtoreth also called Astarte, or Ashtoreth (plural)

Goddess of the Canaanites that related to fertility and maternity. Worship of Ashtoreth was active at Sidon. She was considered the companion of Baal. King Solomon was influenced by his foreign wives and fell into Ashtoreth worship.

Baal sometimes called Bel

Baal was the supreme god among the Canaanites. He was believed to make the earth bear crops, and women bear children. Baal worship included temple prostitution and at times, human sacrifice.

Chemosh

Chemosh was the god of the Moabites. Its ritual frequently involved a human sacrifice. Solomon built an altar to Chemosh south of the Mount of Olives outside Jerusalem, on the Hill of Corruption, 2 Kings 23:13.

Dagon

It was a god of the Philistines. Dagon was a god that governed the water and grain. It statue had the body of a fish with a human head and hands. Samson met his death at the temple of Dagon. According to 1 Samuel 5:1-5, the Philistines captured the ark of the covenant by defeating Israel at the battle of Ebenezer. The Philistine placed the Ark of the Covenant in their temple next to Dagon. The next day the Dagon statue had fallen to the floor. They set it upright, and the following morning it was laying on the floor, face down to the ground before the Ark of the Lord, with the head, and both palms of the hands were broken off with only the stump left, 1 Samuel 5:1-5. According to 1 Chronicles 10:1-10, the Philistines fought against Israel at Mount Gilboa. Saul was wounded in battle and then fell on his own sword. The Philistine placed King Saul's armor in the house of their gods and hung his severed head in the temple of Dagon.

Question: What was in the Ark of the Covenant?

Answer in the back of book

Egyptian Gods

Biblical Egypt had more than 40 false gods, but none are mentioned by name in the Bible. The Hebrews were not tempted to worship these gods during their 400 plus years of captivity in Egypt. The 10 biblical plagues of God performed by Aaron at the command of Moses were against 10 different Egyptian's gods, Exodus chapters 7 through 12.

Golden Calf

The first golden calve was at the foot of Mount Sinai, and it was fashioned by Aaron. The second golden calve was during the reign of King Jeroboam, 1 Kings 12:26-30. In both instances, the golden calves were an idol made by the Israelites. Idols were seen by God as sin, since the 1st and 2nd commandments says, "You shall have no other gods before Me" and "You shall not make idols."

Marduk

Marduk is a god of ancient Mesopotamia, the chief god of the city of Babylon. Marduk was associated with water, fertility, and vegetation.

Milcom

Milcom is the god of the Ammonites. He is associated with divination, seeking knowledge of the future through occult means. Child sacrifice was involved with Milcom rites. He was one of the false gods worshiped by Solomon at the close of his reign. Moloch, Molech, and Molek are variations of this false god name.

During 1 Kings, the period of the prophets is introduced by the great Elijah. First Kings ends with the story of this prophet and second Kings center around his successor, Elisha. Ancient Israel was the promised land of God's chosen people. King David was a mighty warrior. He subdued Israel's enemies and ushered in an era of peace and prosperity.

David's son, Solomon, received extraordinary wisdom from God. He built a magnificent temple in Jerusalem which became the central place of worship. He increased trade and became the wealthiest man of his era. However, Solomon had many foreign wives, who eventually leads him away from the singular worship of Jehovah.

Israel's kings failed to destroy all the shrines built for false gods throughout the land of Israel. The prophets of Baal were allowed to flourish which lead the people astray, and eventually to destruction.

Elijah the prophet severely warned the people of God's wrath over their disobedience, but the kings, rulers, and people would not repent and acknowledge their sins.

The leading individuals in the book of 1 Kings are King David, Solomon, Rehoboam, Jeroboam, Elijah, Ahab, and Queen Jezebel. A brief outline of 1 Kings is listed below:

The Splendid Reign of Solomon – 1 Kings chapter 1-10

1. David's Death, Solomon Ascent as King, 1 Kings 1-2
2. Solomon's Wisdom and Government, 1 Kings 3-4
3. Building and Dedicating the Temple and Palace, 1 Kings 5-8
4. Solomon's Wives and his Downfall, 1 Kings 9-10

The Kingdom Torn Asunder – 1 Kings chapter 11-16

5. Taxes under Solomon's reign weighed the people down, 1 Kings 11
6. Northern Tribes Revolt, 1 Kings 12-13

7. The Acts of the Kings of Israel and Judah, 1 Kings 14-16

The Ministry of Elijah – 1 Kings 17 – 22; 2 Kings 1:1-2:2

8. Ministry of Elijah, 1 Kings 17-21
9. Kings of Israel and Judah, Ahab's death, 1 Kings 22

The Ministry of Elisha – 2 Kings 1 - 9
The Corruption of Israel – 2 Kings 1 - 17
The Captivity of Judah – 2 Kings 13 - 25

In speaking, Solomon's book of Ecclesiastes tells of his mistakes and regrets. A sequence of kings follows Solomon, mostly weak and idolatrous. Israel was once a unified kingdom that becomes divided. The worst of the kings was Ahab, along with his queen, Jezebel. They encouraged the worship of Baal the Canaanite depicted holding a lightning bolt. Baal rituals involved prostitution in the temple. His female companion was Ashtoreth. This brought a great showdown between the prophet Elijah and the prophets of Baal on Mount Carmel.

After Baal's false prophets were slain, Jezebel swore revenge against Elijah, but it was God who imposed punishment. According to 1 Kings 22, Ahab was killed in battle with the Syrians, and approximately 10 years later Jezebel was thrown out of her own palace window by her eunuchs, trampled by horses and eaten by wild dogs, 2 Kings 9.

CHAPTER 2

1ˢᵗ Kings 19:1-18

Chapter 2 contains the passage of Scriptures which this book is the subject of. The words which are in bold print will be discussed in the future chapters. Let's read this passage of Scriptures three times, slowly. May the Lord bless the readers of His Most Holy Word.

Elijah Flees to **Horeb**

When Ahab got home in Jezreel, he told Jezebel everything **Elijah** had done, including the way he had all the prophets of Baal slain with the sword. **Jezebel** immediately sent a messenger with this message to Elijah: "May the gods strike me and even kill me if by this time tomorrow I have not killed you as you killed them."

Elijah was afraid and fled for his life. When he came to Beersheba, a town in Judah, he left his servant there. Then he went a day's journey alone into the wilderness, traveling all day. Elijah came to a **broom tree**, and sat down under it and prayed that he might die. "I have had enough, Lord," he said. "Take my life, I am no better than my ancestors who have already died." Then he lay down and slept under the broom tree.

All at once, while Elijah was sleeping, **an angel touched** him and told him, "Get up and eat!" He looked around and there beside his head was some bread baked on hot coals and a jar of water! So, he ate and drank and then lay down again.

The angel of the Lord came back a second time and touched him and said, "Get up and eat some more, for the journey ahead will be too much for you." So, Elijah got up and ate and drank, and the food gave him enough strength to travel **forty days and forty nights** to Mount Sinai (Horeb), the mountain of God. There he went into a cave, where he spent the night.

The Lord Speaks to Elijah

But the Lord said to him, "What are you doing here, Elijah?"

Elijah replied, "I have been very zealous for the Lord God Almighty. But the people of Israel have rejected your covenant, torn down your altars, and killed every one of your prophets. I am the only one left, and now they are trying to kill me, too."

The Lord said, "Go out and stand before me on the mountain in the presence of the Lord, for the Lord is about to pass by. And as Elijah stood there, the Lord passed by, and a mighty windstorm hit the mountain. It was such a terrible blast that the rocks were torn loose, but the Lord was not in the wind. After the wind, there was an earthquake, but the Lord was not in the earthquake. And after the earthquake, there was a fire, but the Lord was not in the fire. And after the fire, there was the sound of **a gentle whisper**. When Elijah heard it, he wrapped his face in his cloak and went out and stood at the entrance of the cave.

And a voice said, "What are you doing here, Elijah?"

He replied again, "I have zealously served the Lord God Almighty. But the people of Israel have broken their covenant with you, torn down your altars, and killed every one of your prophets. I am the only one left, and now they are trying to kill me, too."

Then the Lord told him, "Go back the same way you came and go to the **Desert of Damascus**. When you arrive there, **anoint Hazael** to be king of Aram (Syria). Then **anoint Jehu** grandson of Nimshi to be king of Israel, and **anoint Elisha** son of Shaphat from the town of Abel-Meholah to succeed you as my prophet. Anyone who escapes from Hazael will be killed by Jehu, and those who escape Jehu will be killed by Elisha! Yet I will reserve **7,000** others in Israel who have never bowed down to Baal and whose mouths have not kissed him!"

CHAPTER 3

Elijah

Elijah name means "My Lord is Jehovah" in Hebrew. He was a fiery Israelite prophet, as well as a miracle worker. Elijah's battles were against the foreign gods which the king had allowed to be worship by the people, with the chief god being Baal and his priestly representatives.

First Kings 17:1 describes, Elijah as "the Tishbite, from Tishbe in Gilead," besides coming from the village of Tishbe, nothing else is known about Elijah's background. Suddenly, he appeared to defend the worship of Jehovah, the God of Israel over those of the Phoenicians, Canaanites, and Sidonians.

Note of Interests: The Phoenicians were the same as the Canaanites, under which name they are known in the Old Testament, as well as Sidonians.

~~~

Elijah lived in the northern kingdom known as Israel during the reigns of King Ahab, Ahaziah, and Jehoram; the first-half of the 9th BC. The biblical accounts of Elijah's life and deeds are recorded in 1st and 2nd Kings. It was half-way through the reign of King Ahab, Elijah makes his first appearance.

King Ahab had formed strong ties with the Phoenician country. The Phoenicians were a remarkable race, seafaring peoples of the ancient world, but they were idolaters. Their main gods of many were Baal and Ashtaroth, which had their own priests and priestesses. The Phoenicians regarded "Jehovah" as only a local deity which they called "The God of the Land."

King Ahab soon became lax in maintaining strict religious practices in Israel. King Ahab went on to marry Jezebel, a Phoenician princess, the daughter of the king of Sidon and the worshippers of foreign gods. As a Jew, Ahab sinned against his Israel faith when he married Jezebel, the daughter of a man whose name, Ethbaal, means, "A Man of Baal." First Kings 16:31 says, she was "Sidonian," which is a biblical term for "Phoenicians," in general.

King Ahab allowed his wife to promote her religious beliefs in Israel. She persecuted the prophets of Jehovah and had many killed. She built two heathen sanctuaries for Baal and Ashtaroth. One shrine of 450 priests was in Samaria, and another 400 priests were housed at Jezreel.

Baal worship was associated with cruel and licentious rites. Baal worship rituals involved prostitution in the temple. For these reasons along with others, King Ahab has been considered as one of the worst of the Israelite Kings.

Elijah is a prophet who purpose was to call the Israelites back to the worship of Jehovah, and away from the evil pagan religious beliefs and practices that were spreading in the land.

Elijah first confrontation with King Ahab is recorded in 1 Kings 17. Elijah appeared before King Ahab to announce God's punishment. Elijah declares to King Ahab that a severe drought would begin, immediately. Elijah said to Ahab, "As the Lord God of Israel lives, before whom I stand, there shall no dew nor rain these years, except at my word." The withholding of rain for 3 ½ years was the first miracle God performed through the prophet Elijah. If there is no rain throughout the kingdom, it will bring a severe famine. The purpose of this punishment was to bring the nation to repentance of its idolatry.

After Elijah told King Ahab this, the Lord told Elijah to flee to a brook called Cherith, located east of the Jordan River. There Elijah drank from the brook, and the Lord commanded the ravens to bring him bread and meat in the morning and in the evening, 1 Kings 17:1-7. After a while, the brook dried up because there was no rainfall anywhere in the land. God then sent Elijah to live in Zarephath, and there he met a widow. God performed another miracle through Elijah there. He blessed the woman's oil and flour, so it did not run out.

While Elijah was there, the widow's son became sick and died. Elijah took the child body from her arms, carried him upstairs, laid him on his bed. Elijah cried out to the Lord, then stretched himself over the child's body three times, and God restored the child's life. The woman told Elijah, "Now I know for sure that you are a man of God and the Lord truly speaks through you," 1 Kings 17:24.

In the third year of the drought, the Lord sent Elijah back to King Ahab. When Ahab saw Elijah, he called him a troublemaker of Israel, 1 Kings 18:17. Elijah told Ahab to summon all the people of Israel and the prophets to Mount Carmel, along with the 450 prophets of Baal and the 400 prophets of the god Asherah, 1 Kings 18:19-20.

Elijah asked the people how long would they be divided between two opinions? Elijah then said, to the people of Israel, if the Lord is God, follow Him; but if Baal is God, then follow him. Elijah had the people to bring two bulls to him. One for Baal and the other for the Lord God. Elijah said the God who answers by fire, He is God, and the people agreed.

The prophets of Baal sacrificed a bull and cried out to Baal from morning until nightfall. They even slashed their skin until blood flowed, but nothing happened. Elijah then repaired the altar of the Lord, took twelve stones to represent each of the tribes of Israel; the sons of Jacob. Elijah then dug a trench about three feet wide around the altar. Elijah set the wood in place, cut the young bull into pieces and laid it on the wood. Elijah had four barrels of water pour over the bull and the wood, 3 times; which is a total of 12 barrels of water.

Elijah walked up to the altar and called on the Lord. Immediately, fire flashed from heaven and consumed the young bull, the wood, and the altar. It also consumed the water and even the dust around it. The people fell on their faces, shouting, "Jehovah is God! Jehovah is God!" 1 Kings 18:39.

Elijah ordered the people to take hold of the false prophets of Baal, and don't let none of them escape. They seized them all, and they took them down to the river Kishon and killed them there. Next, Elijah went up to the top of Mount Carmel and got down on his knees, with his face between his knees, and prayed for rain.

Elijah sent his servant to see if he saw rain coming seven times. On the seventh time, Elijah's servant said he saw a small cloud as small as a man hand rising out of the sea. The sky turned black with clouds, and the wind begins to blow, and there was a great rain, 1 Kings 18:41-45.

Notes of Interest: The prayer Elijah prayed, "Lord, the God of Abraham, Isaac, and Israel, let it be known today that you are God in Israel and that I am your servant and have done all these things at your command. Answer me, Lord, answer me, so these people will know that you, Lord, are God and that you are turning their hearts back again," 1st Kings 18:36-37 NIV.

~~~

When Ahab told Jezebel all that Elijah had done, she was furious at the loss of her prophets and swore to kill him. Jezebel sent a threating message to Elijah by her messenger, telling him she was going to kill him. Elijah became afraid and ran a day journey into the Desert of Damascus wilderness, and sat under a broom tree. Elijah, in his despair, asked God to take his life. While the prophet slept, an angel touched him, brought him food and a jar of water. Elijah ate and then lay down again. The angel of the Lord came back a second time and told him to eat and drink, again. Elijah was strengthened, and Elijah went 40 days and 40 nights to Mount Horeb, where God spoke to Elijah in a whisper.

God tells Elijah to anoint his successor, Elisha, who he found in his father field plowing with 12 yokes of oxen. Elisha made a sacrifice and followed his master, Elijah. Elijah went on to prophesy the deaths of King Ahab, King Ahaziah, and Jezebel.

Question: Who were the other two men God told Elijah to anoint?

1. _____
2. _____

Answer in the back of book

When Elijah and Elisha were on their way from Gilgal, the God sent chariots and horses of fire and took Elijah up to heaven in a whirlwind. Elisha stood watching. Elisha then picked up Elijah's cloak that had fallen from him and went back and stood on the bank of Jordan, 2 Kings 2:11-13.

Notes of Interests: Jewish tradition believes that Elijah is not dead, but continues to wander the earth and will reappear once again when it's time to announce the arrival of the Messiah. Because of this belief, many early Christians thought that John the Baptist was Elijah because John announced the arrival of Jesus.

~~~

Question: Who's another person in the Bible that says he did not die?

Answer in the back of the book

A brief outline of Elijah's miracles and miraculous events are listed below.

Declares a drought, 1 Kings 17:1
Fed by ravens, 1 Kings 17:2-6
Multiplies the widow's flour and oil, 1 Kings 17:7-16
Resurrects the widow's son, 1 Kings 17:17-24
Drought ends after 3 years, 1 Kings 18:1
Call down fire from heaven on Mt. Carmel, 1 Kings 18:1-40
Sent a rainstorm, 1 Kings 18:41-45
Outran a chariot, 1 Kings 18:46
Fed by an angel, 1 Kings 19:4-8
Had a talk with the Lord, 1 Kings 19:11-14
Predicts Ahaziah's death, 2 Kings 1:1-2
Parted the Jordan River, 2 Kings 2:1-8
Ahaziah's men killed by fire from heaven, 2 Kings 1:9-27
At the end of Elijah's life, he went directly to heaven in a whirlwind, 2 Kings 2:11

Elijah's name is mentioned approximately 31 times in the NLT New Testament. The Apostle James speaks of Elijah's prayer and faith. He said,

> **"Elijah was as human as we,**
> **and yet when he prayed earnestly**
> **that no rain would fall,**
> **none fell for three years and a half year!**
> **Then, when he prayed again,**
> **the sky sent down rain,**
> **and the earth began to yield its crops.**
> James 5:17-18 NLT

CHAPTER 4

Horeb

Mount Horeb is a mountain sometimes identified with Mount Sinai. It's located in the Sinai Peninsula of Egypt. Mount Horeb is about 7,487 feet high which is approximately 1½ miles, 2 miles long and 1-mile wide. It's surrounded by higher mountain peaks on all sides. Mount Horeb is a general name for the whole mountain range in which Sinai is considered one of the peaks, by some scholars.

Mount Horeb is considered one of the most important sacred places in the Jewish, Christian and Islamic religions. Mount Horeb is expressed as "the mountain of God," in two verses in the Bible, Exodus 3:1 and 1 Kings 19:8.

However, the phrase "the mountain of God" is mentioned a total of 8 times, only in the Old Testament. It is mentioned in the books of Exodus, 1 Kings, Job, and Ezekiel. Those verses are listed below.

Exodus 3:1 Moses and the Burning Bush.
Moses was tending his father-in-law flock. He led the flock far west of the desert and came to Mount Horeb, also called Sinai, the mountain of God.

Exodus 4:27 Moses Returns to Egypt
Now the Lord told Aaron, "Go out into the wilderness to meet Moses." So, Aaron went and met Moses at the mountain of God, and embraced him.

Exodus 18:5 Jethro's Visit to Moses
Jethro, Moses' father-in-law, came to visit Moses in the wilderness. He brought Moses' wife and two sons with him. They arrived while Moses and the people of Israel were camped near the mountain of God.

Exodus 24:13 Israel Affirms the Lord's Covenant
So, Moses and his assistant Joshua set out, and Moses climbed up the mountain of God.

1 Kings 19:8 Elijah Flees to Horeb
Elijah got up, ate and drank. The food he ate gave him enough strength to travel forty days and forty nights to Mount Horeb, "the mountain of God."

Job 37:22 Elihu Reminds Job of God's Majesty
So also, golden splendour comes from the mountain of God. He is clothed in dazzling splendor.

Ezekiel 28:14 The Lord Prophecy Against the King of Tyre
I ordained and anointed you as the mighty angelic guardian. You were on God's holy mountain and walked among the stones of fire.

Ezekiel 28:16 The Lord Prophecy Against the King of Tyre

By the abundance of your global trade, led you to violence, and you sinned. So, I drove you in disgrace from the mountain of God, and expelled you, O mighty guardian, from your place among fiery stones.

Although Mount Sinai and Mount Horeb are different names, they are often considered being the same place. There are others who think that they are different places. Jewish and Christian scholars have varying opinions as to its whereabouts since biblical times.

John Calvin, a Protestant reformer believed that Mount Sinai and Horeb were the same mountains. The eastern side of the mountain being called Sinai and the western side called Horeb. On the north-east side of the mountain is where the Israelites camped for nearly a year, after the Exodus from Egypt.

The name Horeb is mentioned first in Exodus 3:1 surrounding Moses and the burning bush. The biblical event is described as follows. Moses was pasturing the flock of Jethro, who was the priest of Midian, and his father-in-law. When Moses led the flock to the west side of the desert, he came to Horeb, "the mountain of God." An angel of the Lord appeared to Moses in a fiery flame of fire from within the bush. Moses looked and lo, the bush was burning, yet it was not consumed. And Moses said, "I will go and see this great sight, why the bush is not burnt." When the Lord saw that Moses had turned aside to see, God called to him out of the midst of the burning bush. God said, "Moses, Moses!" And Moses said, "Here am I."

The Lord then told Moses, "Don't come near, take his sandals off his feet, because the place on which he was standing is holy ground." The Lord further said, "I am the God of your father, the God of Abraham, the God of Isaac, and the God of Jacob," Exodus 3:1-6.

It was at mountain Horeb, God told Moses, he had seen the misery of his people in Egypt, heard their cry, know their sorrows and suffering. The Lord told Moses, He had come down to deliver them from the hands of the Egyptian and bring them to their own fertile, good and spacious land. God told Moses, he was sending him to Pharaoh to deliver the Israelites from out of Egypt.

After the Exodus, the congregation of the Israelites left the desert of Sin, and they moved from place to place. They eventually camped at Rephidim, where there was no water to drink, the people were suffering from thirst. They were complaining to Moses. God told Moses to take some elders of Israel with him and strike a rock with his staff at Mount Horeb. When Moses struck the rock as he was told, water gushed out, as the elders looked on, Exodus 17:1-6.

Notes of Interests: Exodus 17:7 KJV reads, "And he (Moses) called the name of the place Massah, and Meribah, because of the chiding of the children of Israel, and because they tempted the Lord, saying, Is the Lord among us, or not? Massah means "test" and Meribah means "arguing."

~~~

After breaking camp at Rephidim, the Israelites set up camp at the base of Mount Horeb. The Israelites were told from this mountain they would receive the commandments of God and they would hear His very voice. They were given two days for preparation, and on the third day God would come down on Mount Horeb in the sight of all the people.

Moses set boundaries at the foot of the mountain because the people were prohibited from touching Mount Horeb. If anyone touched Mount Horeb, the penalty was death by stoning, or they would be shot with an arrow.

On the third day, there was lightning, thundering, and a loud trumpet blast along with a thick cloud over the mountain. Everyone in the camp trembled as Moses led the people out of the camp to meet with God, and they stood at the foot of the mountain. God then spoke the Ten Commandments to the people.

Mount Horeb was covered in a cloud of smoke for six days because the Lord descended upon it in a fire. On the seventh day, God commanded Moses to climb Mount Horeb to receive the tables of the Law. Moses remained there forty days and nights, Exodus 24:18.

Horeb is the mountain where Moses fast twice for forty days, Exodus 24:18 and Exodus 34:28. It's where he receives the Ten Commands chisel out of two stone tablets, written by the finger of God, Exodus 31:18.

Horeb is mentioned several times in the book of Deuteronomy in the accounts of the wanderings of the Israelites in the wilderness by Moses. He recalled what God had said to the Israelites at Mount Horeb.

**The Lord our God said to us at Horeb,
"You have stayed long enough at this mountain."**
Deuteronomy 1:6 NIV

Mount Horeb is where the Israelites set off to Canaanite to possess the land the Lord had promised to their forefathers.

The accounts of Moses and the Ten Commandments at Mount Horeb are mentions in Deuteronomy 4.

According to Deuteronomy 5:2, Moses reminds the people of the covenant they made with God at Mount Horeb. How God spoke to them face to face from the heart of the fire.

In Deuteronomy 9:8, Moses tells the people not to forget how angry the Lord God was at Mount Horeb and wanted to destroy them.

In Deuteronomy 18:16, Moses tells the people God will raise up a prophet like him from among the Israelites. He tells them this is what they asked for at Mount Horeb.

The terms of the covenant the Lord commanded Moses to make with the Israelites while they were in the land of Moab, in addition to the covenant he had made with them at Mount Horeb are recording in Deuteronomy 29.

Deuteronomy 33:2 records the blessing that Moses gave the people of Israel before his death: "The Lord came from Mount Sinai and dawned upon us from Mount Seir; he shone forth from Mount Paran and came from Meribah-Kadesh with flaming fire at his right hand." NLT

Other verses that mention Mount Horeb are listed below.

Psalms 106, refers to the Israelites at Mount Horeb when they made a golden calf and worshipped the molten image.

The prophet Malachi tells Israel to, "Remember ye the law of Moses, my servant, which I commanded unto him in Horeb for all Israel, with the statutes and judgments," Malachi 4:4.

1 Kings 8:9 and 2 Chronicles 5:10, states that the Ark of the Covenant contained only the tablets were delivered to Moses at Horeb.

1 Kings 19:8, Elijah flees to "Horeb, the mount of God." Elijah spends forty days and nights fasting on Mount Horeb, 1 Kings 19:8. Afterward, he has his famous conversation with God, 1 Kings 19:9-18.

CHAPTER 5

Jezebel

Jezebel was a Phoenician Princess of Sidon in the 9th century. According to 1 Kings 16:31 she was "Sidonian" which is a biblical term for Phoenicians, in general. Jezebel was taught to worship many gods, and the chief god was named Baal and Ashtoreth was his consort.

According to genealogies given by first-century Jewish historian Titus Flavius Josephus, Jezebel was the great-aunt of Dido, Queen of Carthage. She was the daughter of Ethbaal from Tyre, king of the Phoenician empire, who also served as a high priest for the god Ashtoreth, the primary Phoenician goddess. The name Ashtoreth is also spelled Astarte.

The Phoenicians were a group of Semites whose ancestors were Canaanites. They established cities and colonies which included sophisticated maritime trade centers for Tyre and Sidon on the Mediterranean coast. The Phoenicians worshiped many gods and goddesses. The chief god among the many was Baal. The name Baal means "lord." He was the fertility and agricultural god of the Canaanites.

The Books of Kings records princess Jezebel being brought to Israel, the northern kingdom to wed the newly crowned king; Ahab, the son of Omri. In those days, there was the ever-present menace of Syria and the growing threat of Assyria. King Ahab made an alliance with his neighboring nations. He made a treaty with the king of Phoenicia and sealed it by marrying his daughter, Jezebel. Israel was at peace during much of King Ahab's reign.

Ahab marriage to Jezebel helped his friendship with Tyre, and his alliance with Jehoshaphat, king of Judah. This union provided them with both military protection from powerful enemies, as well as valuable trade routes. The Kingdom of Israel gained access to the Phoenician ports, and Phoenicia was granted passage through Israel's central hill country, and especially to the King's Highway.

The King's Highway was an important road running N and S from Damascus to the Gulf of Aqabah, and E of the Dead Sea and the Jordan Valley.

Notes of Interests: A reference to the "King's Highway" is mentioned in Numbers 20:17, Numbers 21:22, and Deuteronomy 2:27. Moses requested permission to travel the King's Highway when passing through the territory of the Edomites, and of Sihon, the Amorite king. Moses promised to keep strictly to the road while passing through. It was one of the most important routes for international commerce. The King's Highway ran through Bashan, Gilead, Ammon, Moab, and Edom, and connected with roads across the Negeb leading into Egypt. The King's Highway route of travel is known to have existed well before 2000 BC.

~ ~ ~

Jezebel is married to King Ahab when ancient Israel was torn into two nations; Israel the north, and Judah the south. Ahab was King of Israel from 874 to 853 BC, the son, and successor of Omri. He led the northern Kingdom of Israel to great power and established Samaria as his capital.

However, Ahab's wife, Jezebel worshipped pagan gods. When she came to Israel, she brought her gods and goddesses with her from her native land; especially Baal and his consort Asherah, often translated in the Bible as "sacred post." She encouraged the Israelites to worship Baal. Jezebel, as a king's daughter, probably served as a priestess in the temple as she was growing-up and she was undoubtedly loyal to these pagan deities.

King Ahab built a sanctuary for Baal in the capital city of Samaria. Ahab also made sacred posts which he served and worshiped, 1 Kings 16. Jezebel organized and maintained guilds of prophets; 450 for Baals and 400 for Asherah. She had many prophets of Israel killed. Obadiah, the prophet, and overseer of Ahab's house rescued 100 prophets that Jezebel was trying to kill, by hiding them in a cave and secretly feeding them.

Notes of Interests: Around this time, Athaliah, the daughter of King Ahab and Queen Jezebel of Israel was the wife of King Jehoram of Judah. Athaliah had been given to Jehoram to seal a treaty between the two sometimes warring nations of Judah and Israel. Athaliah, the Queen of Judah worshipped pagan gods, too. She was the only ruling queen of Judah or Israel, and she reigned for 6 years. After Jehoram's death, their son Ahaziah became Judah's king. During a visit to Israel, Ahaziah was murdered by Jehu, along with Athaliah's mother, Jezebel. Athaliah countered a bloody coup in Jerusalem, placing herself on the throne and attempting to eliminate any possible royal heir. The high priest Jehoiada hid and nurtured Athaliah's grandson Jehoash. When the time was right, Jehoiada overthrew and executed Athaliah, and placed Jehoash on the throne in her place. Jehoash was seven years old when he begins to reign. Jehoash is also known as Joash and Joas.

~~~

At this significant moment, Elijah, a Jewish prophet, appeared. According to 1st Kings 17, Elijah prophesied to King Ahab that there would be no dew or ran in the years to come. The Lord told Elijah to leave and traveled eastward and hide out in the Cherith Valley. The drought came upon Israel resulting in a famine across the land.

In the third year of the famine, the Lord sent Elijah back to Ahab. Elijah had King Ahab to summon all the prophets of Baal at Mount Carmel for a challenge of whose god is indeed God. It was agreed upon that the god who answered his prophet by fire, is the "One True God."

The prophets of Baal and Elijah set up two altars. Baal's prophets called on Baal, and he didn't answer them. Elijah won the challenge because when he called on Jehovah, God sent fire from heaven which burnt the sacrifice. The prophets of Baal were immediately killed by the Israelites. When Ahab told Jezebel of the slaughter, she angrily swore to have Elijah killed, and he fled for his life, 1 Kings 18 and 19.

The story of Naboth the Jezreelite is one of the well-known stories in Jezebel's life. Naboth was a landowner who lived close to the King's palace. Naboth was asked to sell his land by King Ahab. Naboth refused to sell his family's ancestral land. Inflamed by Naboth's refusal to King Ahab, Jezebel had him falsely charged him with treason and blaspheming "God and the king." Naboth was condemned to death by stoning. Queen Jezebel afterward took Naboth land for the king.

At this time, Elijah arrived and confronted King Ahab about this transgression. He prophesied that Ahab's descendants would be killed and the flesh of Jezebel corpses would be eaten by stray dogs.

Several years later, Ahab died in a battle against the Syrians at Ramoth-Gilead. He was succeeded by his first son, Ahaziah, but he died because of an accident.

Notes of Interests: Ahaziah was in his palace when he suffered a severe fall. He sent servants to Ekron to ask advice of their idol god, Baalzebub, would he recover? Elijah stopped the messengers and sent them back to the king with this message, "Are you consulting a foreign idol because there is no God in Israel? For this offense, you will not recover, but die!" King Ahaziah then sent 50 officers to arrest Elijah. But Elijah refused to be arrested and called fire from heaven to consume them. Ahaziah sent a second group of 50 men, and they were consumed, as well.

Ahaziah sent a third group of 50 men to arrest Elijah. By knowing the fate of the first two groups, they didn't try to arrest Elijah. Instead, they respectfully requested Elijah to accompany them. Elijah decided to go with them. When he met the king, Elijah delivered the same message that he had sent to the king that he would die. Ahaziah had no sons, so he was succeeded by his brother Jehoram, 1 Kings 22, 2 Kings 1, and 2 Chronicles 20.

~~~

Ahaziah was succeeded by his brother, Joram. Joram name is also spelled Jehoram.

Notes of Interests: According to 2 Kings 8:16, in the 5th year of Joram of Israel, (another), Jehoram became king of Judah. The book of Kings speaks of both Jehoram of Israel and Jehoram of Judah in the same passage, which can be confusing.

~~~

According to 2 Kings 9, Elisha sent a young prophet to anoint Jehu, the commander of Joram's army, to be king over Israel. He was ordered at this time to destroy Ahab's descendants as a punishment for the evil ways Jezebel had treated God's prophets and people. In 1 Kings 19, Elijah was told by God to anoint Hazael, Jehu, and his successor Elisha.

Jehu killed Jehoram(Joram) at the site of Naboth's vineyard and then went to the royal palace at Jezreel, where Jezebel lived. As the story goes, when Jehu made his way to Jezebel's palace to murder her. She appears to be expecting him. She had applied makeup to her face and was dressed in her most beautiful apparel sitting in her window. Jezebel actions have been interpreted in a variety of ways. Some people believe she was merely dressing for a dignified death. Others think she had dressed and painted herself in hopes of seducing Jehu.

In the end, Jehu ordered her eunuchs to throw Jezebel out of her bedroom window. Her blood spattered on the wall and on the horses, that trampled on her body. When Jehu ordered Jezebel's body to be taken up for a proper burial, Jehu's servants discovered only her skull, her feet and the palms of her hands. Jezebel's flesh had been eaten by stray dogs, fulfilling Elijah prophecy. Jezebel's death is dated to 850 BC.

The name Jezebel has been used for thousands of years to describe cunning, heartless and deplorable women. Her name is also synonymous with idolaters, prostitutes, and sorcerers. Since her death, she has become legendary.

Jezebel did not worship Ahab's God, Jehovah; she leads Ahab to worship Baal. Jezebel consistently remains true to her own beliefs. This ancient queen has been publicly declared a murderer, prostitute, and an enemy of God.

Jezebel is viewed as a woman who is opposite to Ruth the Moabite, who was also a foreigner. She surrenders her identity and submerges herself in Israel ways. Ruth adopts the religious of the Israelites and is widely praised for her conversion to God.

Jezebel is not a warrior like Deborah, a loving sister like Miriam or a caring wife like Ruth. Jezebel cannot even be compared to the list of bad girls in the Bible; like Potiphar's wife or Delilah. These women may be considered evil, but Jezebel is the worst of the worst.

The biblical events that surround Jezebel are found in 1 Kings, chapters 16, 18, 19, 21, and 2 Kings chapter 9. In the New Testament, Jezebel's name is used symbolically as a false prophetess who seeks to lure Christians into idolatrous practice, Revelation 2.

Nevertheless, I have this against you:
You tolerate that woman Jezebel,
who calls herself a prophet.
By her teaching,
she misleads my servants into sexual immorality
and the eating of food sacrificed to idols.
Revelation 2:20 NIV

Question: Which of the seven churches were Revelation 2:20 directed to?

_____ 1. The Church in Ephesus
_____ 2. The Church in Smyrna
_____ 3. The Church in Pergamum
_____ 4. The Church in Thyatira
_____ 5. The Church in Sardis
_____ 6. The Church in Philadelphia
_____ 7. The Church in Laodicea

Answer in the back of book

CHAPTER 6

Broom Tree

Beginning at the first book of the Bible, up to the last book of the Bible, trees are essential to mankind. A tree was involved with man's sin. According to Genesis 3:1-7, Adam and Eve ate from the forbidden fruit of the tree of knowledge of good and evil in the Garden of Eden. Another tree was involved in the price of man's sin being paid because the Lord Jesus Christ died by crucifixion upon a tree at Calvary.

A few events, people and places associated with trees are listed below:

1. God placed the cherubim and a flaming sword to guard the way to the Tree of Life, Genesis 3:24.
2. Jacob cut fresh branches from Poplar, Almond and Plane Trees and peeled white stripes on them to expose the white inner wood of the branches, Genesis 30:37.
3. Deborah sat under a Palm Tree as a judge, Judges 4:5.
4. King Saul and his army camped on the outskirts of Gibeah under a Pomegranate Tree in Migron, 1 Samuel 14:2.

5. When the Lord asked Jeremiah what do he see? He said, "He saw a branch of an Almond Tree," Jeremiah 1:11.
6. The Ash Tree is mentioned only in Isaiah 44:14.
7. According to Ezekiel 27:6 states, Cypress wood from the coasts of Cyprus they made benches, adorned with ivory.
8. Amos was a dresser of Sycamore Trees, Amos 7:14.

There are many kinds of trees named in the Bible. The trees listed below surrounds renowned biblical events.

The Fig Tree

The Fig Tree is the first type of tree mentioned by name in the Bible, Genesis 3:7. The fig tree became a covering for Adam and Eve. After Adam and Eve have sinned, they used fig leaves to try to hide their sinfulness from the eyes of a searching God, Genesis 3:6-13.

This tree has been labeled a hypocrite tree because the fruit is green before it ripens. It cannot be easily seen among the leaves until it is nearly ripe. Only when you look closely can the fruit be detected in its early stages. According to Mark 11:12-20, Jesus came to a fig tree, desiring fruit, but found only leaves, and He cursed the tree, and it dried up from the roots.

Zacchaeus climbed a sycamore tree so he could see Jesus as he passed that way, Luke 19:1-10. A sycamore tree is a type of fig tree, and a sycamore tree can reach heights of fifty feet or more.

The Gopher Tree

The gopher wood was used to construct the ark. Gopherwood or gopher wood is a term used once in the Bible as the wood to be used to build Noah's ark, Genesis 6:14. It is a word of uncertain, not known in the Bible or in Hebrew. Moses, the author of Genesis, understood its meaning, but it has been lost to time. Scholars believe it to be the tree Torreya taxifolia, sometimes called "gopher wood." The gopher wood is known for its longevity and strength. Noah, his wife, his 3 sons and their wives; eight of them entered the ark.

The Olive Tree

Another valuable tree, especially in the land of Israel was the olive tree. The tree became the biblical symbol for the nation of Israel, Roman 11:15-25. The Olive Tree is known as the emblem of peace, prosperity, and wealth, Psalm 128. Its berries are still one of the leading articles of Israel commerce. When the olive crop fails, it is thought to be a sign of divine wrath, Jeremiah 11:16-23. Olive oil was used in the tabernacle for light and ceremonial anointing by the priests of God, Exodus, 30:24-25, Leviticus 24:2-4. According to the book of Genesis, Noah knew the water on the land had receded, when the dove he had sent out returned to the ark with an olive twig in her beak.

The Oliver Tree needs no irrigation, it thrives well in the Palestinian hills. Olive oil is the primary source of fat for consumption and frying because animal fat cannot be kept for a long time. Olive oil served as a base for all cosmetics and cleaning products. It's used in clay lamps which were the primary source for lighting in Bible days.

Cedar Tree

King Hiram sent cedar and fir trees to Solomon. The cedar trees were used in building the temple of God in Jerusalem, 1 Kings 6:9-20. There are several possible reasons this tree was chosen.

1. The wood is not attacked by insect pests.
2. The tree is free from knots.
3. It has remarkable lasting qualities.

The cedar forests in Lebanon had trees to grew to heights of 120 feet, and the measurement around the middle sometimes measured up to 40 feet. Their lifespan is often over 2,000 years.

The cedars of Lebanon are very rare, now. The cedar tree was used to build the temple of the Lord, Solomon's house, and other public structures in Jerusalem. The cedars of Lebanon were used to roof the temple of Diana at Ephesus and Apollo at Utica.

The Oak Tree

The Oak Tree is another tree known for its longevity. It stood as a witness to specific events in Bible days. Jacob took false idols from the members of the household and buried them under an oak tree at Shechem, Genesis 35:4. It was at an oak tree that Joshua took idols from the nations of Israel, who had promised to serve only the true God, Joshua 24:14-26.

Notes of Interests: The scriptures do not tell us if it was the same oak tree that Jacob and Joshua burned idols, but some scholars presume that it is.

~~~

Abraham pitched his tent under an oak tree in Hebron. The Lord appeared to Abraham near the oak grove belonging to Mamre. Abraham was told by this time next year his wife, Sarah, would have a son. The Angel of the Lord appeared to Gideon under an oak tree in Ophrah, when the land of Israel was oppressed by Midian. There the angel told Gideon, he would deliver Israel from their oppression, Judges 6:11-19.

The heathen worshipped idols in oak groves, Ezekiel 6:13. King David son Absalom died in an oak tree, 2 Samuels 18:6-17. King Saul was buried under an oak tree, 1 Chronicles 10:12.

The Broom Tree

The biblical events of Elijah and the broom tree is recorded in 1 Kings Chapters 18 and 19, and it occurred during the reign of King Ahab, who reigned from 874-853 BC.

In brief, Elijah challenged King Ahab and the prophets of Baal to see which God would answer his prophet(s) with fire. Ahab gathered all of Baal prophets and met Elijah on Mount Carmel. Many of the Israelites were present to watch the outcome.

The prophets of Baals cut up a bull and placed it on an altar dedicated to Baal. They called on Baal to ignite the sacrifice with fire from heaven. Despite calling on Baal from morning until evening and slashing themselves, the sacrifice to Baal wasn't consumed by fire.

Elijah cut a bull in pieces and placed it on the altar. A significant amount of water was poured on the bull and altar. Elijah called on the God of Abraham, Isaac, and Jacob. Immediately, fire consumed Elijah's sacrifice. The people fell prostrate and cried, "The Lord, he is God! The Lord, He is God! Elijah commanded, "Seize all the prophets of Baal. Don't let a single one escape!" The people seized them all and killed them in the Kishon Valley, 1 Kings 18:39-40.

After King Ahab told Queen Jezebel what had happened. She then sent a messenger to Elijah, saying that she would kill him by that time tomorrow. Elijah then fled, and when he came to a broom tree, he sat down under it and prayed that he would die. Elijah was completely disheartened, and finally, he fell asleep.

While Elijah was sleeping under the broom tree, an angel touched him. He told Elijah to get up and eat. Elijah looked around and saw a cake of bread baked and a jar of water. After eating Elijah went back to sleep.

The angel touched Elijah a second time and said, "Get up and eat, for the journey," 1 Kings 19:7. Elijah was strengthened by the food, and he traveled 40 days and nights until he reached Mount Horeb. The same mountain where Moses saw the burning bush and where God gave Moses the 10 Commandments of Israel.

In Bible days in Israel, the white broom tree was used for kindling in cooking. The roots, trunks, and branches of the broom trees were used as burning coals because their ashes hold heat for an extended period, even after they appear to be dead ashes.

Desert travelers have been known to form a layer of broom ashes to fix the shape of their body size. They then covered the ashes with 2-4 inch of sand. The sand-covered ashes provided a warm mattress during the chilly desert nights.

The broom tree where Elijah rested under is in the southern part of Israel and was called the Retama raetam. It is also known as the white broom and the white weeping broom tree. The broom tree is a native to the Middle East, North Africa, and Sicily. Even though it is considered a tree, according to Botanist, the broom tree is regarded as an oversized desert shrub with a broad canopy in the juniper family. It's ideal for a desert environment, but during the wet season, it will produce small leaves and even flowers.

In Israel, it is widespread in deserts and the Mediterranean woodlands. The white broom tree is beautiful between January and April when it is covered with countless blooms of white flowers. The flowers give off a soothing honey fragrance.

The broom tree is durable. It represents renewal, and with renewal comes a restoration of robustness and a new freshness. When Elijah arrived at the broom tree, he was exhausted, depressed, and ready to die. Elijah's victory at Mount Carmel over Baal and his prophets turned into Elijah fleeing for his life from Jezebel's wrath. If the shrub were blooming, Elijah would have seen thousands of tiny white flowers and smelled a soothing aroma. After sinking beneath the tree canopy, Elijah fell asleep. The warm embers under the sand may have helped maintain his warmth in the chilly desert night. The broom tree ember ashes were used to bake a cake of bread for Elijah.

Notes of Interests: In the NIV Bible, Broom Tree is referred to as Broom Bush, 1 Kings 19:5. In the NLT Bible Version, the words "Broom Tree" only occurs three times in the Bible in the following verses: 1 Kings 19:4, 1 Kings 19:5 and Job 30:4. In the KJV, the "Broom Tree" is called a "Juniper Tree" and only mentioned in 1 Kings 19:4 and 1 Kings 19:5. The Broom Tree plant is common in the Middle East, especially near Lebanon, Mount Carmel, Gilead, Jordan and the Dead Sea.

~ ~ ~

In summing it all up, "Faith is often strengthened under the broom tree. Where we begin to hear God still quiet voice and surrender our will to Him."

CHAPTER 7

An Angel Touched Him

Then he lay down and slept under the broom tree. But as he was sleeping, an angel touched him and told him, "Get up and eat!" 1 Kings 19:5 NLT

Then the angel of the Lord came again and touched him and said, "Get up and eat some more or the journey ahead will be too much for you." 1 Kings 19:7 NLT

~~~

These are the only two recorded verses in which an angel is mentioned touching anyone, in the Bible. The individual who these verses are referring to is Elijah.

It was noticed that the phrase "the angel of the Lord" occurs 49 times in the Old Testament and 9 times in the New Testament, KJV. While the phrase "an angel of the Lord" only occurs 5 times in the Old Testament and just in the book of Judges, it occurs 3 times in the New Testaments.

Whether it's written, "the angel of the Lord" or "an angel of the Lord" or "angel of God" it is an entity appearing or acting on behalf of God. In some verses, it's clear that the reference is a visible manifestation of God to mankind, rather than a separate entity acting on God's behalf. Based on Luke 1:11-19, the "angel of the Lord" identifies himself as Gabriel, an angel sent from God.

Gabriel was speaking to Zacharias while he was standing at the right side of the altar of incense.

The visible appearance of the "angel of the Lord" is often presented as "theophany." Theophany refers to the appearance of a deity to a human. This word has been used to refer to the appearance of the gods in the ancient Greek and Eastern religions.

The word "theophany" in regards to Christians and Jews refer to the manifestation of God to people and the sign by which the presence of God is revealed.

The Angel of the Lord is identified by some Christians as the pre-incarnate Christ. The word "Angel" in references to "the Angel of the Lord" is capitalized in the Old Testament, KJV, and NKJV. Most versions, including NASB, RSV, ESV do not capitalize the word "angel" in the Old Testament when mentioning "the angel of the Lord."

The following are verses where the phrase **"the angel of God"** appears in the Bible.

Genesis 31:11 NIV   Jacob Flees from Laban
The angel of God said to me in the dream, "Jacob." I answered, "Here I am."

Exodus 14:19 NIV   Escaping the Egyptians and Crossing the Red Sea

Then the angel of God, who had been traveling in front of Israel's army, withdrew and went behind them.

The pillar of cloud also moved from in front and stood behind them.

Judges 13:9 NIV   The Birth of Samson
God listened to Manoah. The angel of God came again to the woman while she was sitting in the field. But Manoah her husband was not with her.

The following are verses where the phrase **"the angel of the Lord"** appears in the Bible.

Genesis 16:9 NLT   Hagar and the Angel of the Lord
And the angel of the Lord said to her, "Return to thy mistress, and submit to her authority.

Genesis 22:11 NLT   God Test Abraham's Faith
At that moment the angel of the Lord called to him from heaven, "Abraham! Abraham!" "Yes," Abraham replied. "Here I am!"

Exodus 3:2 NLT   Moses and the Burning Bush
There the angel of the Lord appeared to him in a blazing fire from the middle of the bush. Moses stared in amazement. Though the bush was engulfed in flames, it didn't burn up.

Numbers 22:23 NLT   Balaam and His Donkey
Balaam's donkey saw the angel of the Lord standing in the road with a drawn sword in his hand. The donkey bolted off the road into a field, but Balaam beat it and turned it back onto the road.

Numbers 22:31 NLT   Balaam, the Donkey, and the Angel

Then the Lord opened Balaam's eyes, and he saw the angel of the Lord standing in the roadway with a drawn sword in his hand. Balaam bowed his head and fell face down on the ground before him.

Judges 2:4 NLT   The Lord's Messenger and Israel's Disobedience

When the angel of the Lord finished speaking to all the Israelites, the people wept loudly.

Judges 6:11-12 NLT   Gideon

Then the angel of the Lord came and sat beneath the great tree at Ophrah, which belonged to Joash of the clan of Abiezer. Gideon son of Joash was threshing wheat at the bottom of a winepress to hide the grain from the Midianites. The angel of the Lord appeared to him and said, "Mighty hero, the Lord is with you!".

Judges 13:3 KJV   The Birth of Samson

And the angel of the Lord appeared unto the woman, and said unto her, Behold now, thou art barren, and bearest not: but thou shalt conceive, and bear a son.

Judges 13:15-16 KJV   Samson's Father and the Angel of the Lord

And Manoah said unto the angel of the Lord, I pray thee, let us detain thee, until we shall have made ready a kid for thee. And the angel of the Lord said unto Manoah,

Though, thou detain me, I will not eat of thy bread: and if thou wilt offer a burnet offering, thou must offer it unto the Lord. For Manoah knew not that he was an angel of the Lord.

Judges 13:20 KJV   Angel of the Lord Ascended
For it came to pass, when the flame went up toward heaven from off the altar, that the angel of the Lord ascended in the flame of the altar. And Manoah and his wife looked on it, and fell on their faces to the ground.

2 Kings 1:15 NLT   Elijah Confronts and Denounces Kings Ahaziah
Then the angel of the Lord said to Elijah, "Go down with him, and don't be afraid of him." So Elijah got up and went with him to the king.

2 Kings 19:35-36 NIV   Isaiah Prophesies Sennacherib's Defeat
That night the angel of the Lord went out and put to death a hundred and eighty-five thousand n the Assyrian camp. When the people got up the next morning-there were all the dead bodies! So Sennacherib king of Assyria broke camp and withdrew. He returned to Nineveh and stayed there.

1 Chronicles 21:16 NLT   Punishment for David's Census of the People
David looked up and saw the angel of the Lord standing between heaven and earth with his sword drawn, reaching

out over Jerusalem. So David and the leaders of Israel put on burlap to show their deep distress and fell face down on the ground., having a drawn sword in his hand stretched out over Jerusalem. Then David and the elders of Israel, who were clothed in sackcloth, fell upon their faces.

Psalm 34:7 NLT   A Psalm of David, regarding the time he pretended t be insane in from of Abimelech, who sent him away.
For the angel of the Lord is a guard; he surrounds and defends all who fear him.

Matthew 1:20 KJV   Joseph and the Birth of Jesus the Messiah
But while he thought on these things, behold, the angel of the Lord appeared unto him in a dream, saying, Joseph thou son of David, fear not to take unto thee Mary thy wife: for that which is conceived in her is of the Holy Ghost.

Matthew 28:2 KJV   The Resurrection of Jesus
And, behold, there was a great earthquake: for the angel of the Lord descended from heaven, and came and rolled back the stone from the door, and sat upon it.

Luke 2:9 KJV   The Shepherds and the Angel
And, lo, the angel of the Lord came upon them, and the glory of the Lord shone round about them: and they were sore afraid.

Acts 5:18-19 NIV   The Apostles Persecuted and Arrested
They arrested the apostles and put them in the public jail. But during the night an angel of the Lord opened the doors of the jail and brought them out.

Acts 8:26 KJV   Philip and the Ethiopian Eunuch
And the angel of the Lord spake unto Philip, saying, Arise, and go toward the south unto the way that goeth down from Jerusalem unto Gaza, which is a desert.

Acts 12:7 KJV   Peter's Miraculous Escape from Prisoned
And, behold, the angel of the Lord came upon him, and a light shined in the prison: and he smote Peter on the side, and raised him up saying, Arise up quickly. And his chains fell off from his hands.

Acts 12:23 KJV   Angel of the Lord Struck Herod Down
And immediately the angel of the Lord smote him, because he gave not God the glory: and he was eaten of worms, and gave up the ghost.

The following are verses where the phrase "**an angel of the Lord**" is mentioned.

Judges 2:1 KJV   Israel is Rebuked by the Angel of the Lord at Bokim
And an angel of the Lord came up from Gilgal to Bochim, and said, I made you to go up out of Egypt, and have brought you unto the land which I sware unto your fathers; and I said, I will never break my covenant with you.

Matthew 2:19-20 KJV   The Return to Nazareth
But when Herod was dead, behold, an angel of the Lord appeareth in a dream to Joseph in Egypt. Saying, Arise, and take the young child and his mother, and go into the land of Israel: for they are dead which sought the young child's life.

Luke 1:11-12 KJV   John the Baptist's Birth Announced to Zacharias
And there appeared unto him an angel of the Lord standing on the right side of the altar of incense. And when Zacharias saw him, he was troubled, and fear fell upon him.

The book of Acts 12:11 and Revelation 22:6 mentions "his angel" which can also be understood as referring either to "the angel of the Lord" or "an angel of the Lord."

Notes of Interests: The following are examples of God "sending an angel."

Exodus 23:20-21. The Lord says he will send an Angel before the Israelites, and warns them to obey the Angel's voice, and that the Angel "will not pardon transgression" because the Lord's "name is in him."

Exodus 33:2. God says he will send an angel before the Israelites, and that God will drive out the Canaanites, Amorites, Hittites, Perizzites, the Hivites, and the Jebusites.

Numbers 20:16. The Lord sent an angel and brought the people of Israel forth from Egypt.

1. Chronicles 21:15. God sent an angel to destroy Jerusalem, but then repented and told the angel to stay his hand.
2. Chronicles 32:21. The Lord sent an angel, which cut off all the mighty men of valour and the leaders and captains in the camp of the king of Assyria.

~~~

It's a good time for a question: How many of the above biblical events are you familiar with in each phrase heading? Why don't you take a few days to refresh your mind, bless your body, spirit and soul by reading or reread them all in the Bible? Hallelujah   *Smile* . . .

"the angel of God" _____
"the angel of the Lord" _____
"an angel of the Lord" _____

CHAPTER 8

Forty Days and Forty Nights

The number 40 coincides with a period of testing in the Bible. It's a number that deals with time. It symbolizes a period of probation, trial, and chastisement. Don't confuse the number 40 with "judgment" which is represented by the number 9.

Note of Interests: The 2nd book in this series is titled: <u>Isaiah 26:3-4 "Perfect Peace" The Last Single Digit</u> published on 02/13/2012 is about the number 9.

~~~

The number 40 appears approximately 84 times in the King James Bible in a context that deals mostly with trials or testing. There are many scholars, who believe it to be the number that represents probation or trial. The number 40 still has a literal meaning in the Bible, and that "forty days" means "forty days."

Several verses in the Bible, describe a period of time as 40 days and 40 nights. The KJV mentions "40 days and 40 nights" a total of 11 times. The Bible also mentions 40 years, quite a bit.

Starting in Genesis, the Lord told Noah to go inside the Ark because it was going to rain for 40 days and 40 nights until He had wiped from the earth all the living things He had created, Genesis 7:1-4.

When Noah was in the Ark, God made it rain for 40 days and 40 nights. Finally, after 150 days, the Ark rested on the Mount Ararat. Noah waited 40 more days before he opened a window in the Ark and released a raven and a dove, Genesis 8:1-8.

According to Genesis 18:1-33, the Lord told Abraham, the outcry against Sodom and Gomorra were great and their sins grievous and He was going to destroy them. Abraham pleads with God not to destroy Sodom and Gomorrah if 40 righteous people could be found. Sodom and Gomorrah were destroyed.

According to Genesis 25:20 and 26:34, both Isaac and Esau were 40 years old when they got married. Isaac married Rebekah, the daughter of Bethuel the Aramean from Paddan-Aram and the sister of Ladan the Aramean. Esau married two Hittite wives who were Judith, the daughter of Beeri, and Basemath, the daughter of Elon.

When the patriarch Jacob died in Egypt, the Egyptians spent 40 days embalming his body, and 70 days mourning his death, Genesis 50:3. This was the Egyptian custom. The 40 days was said to be for the preparation of going into a new life, what they called the afterlife.

Question: What did God change Jacob name to?

_____

Answer in the back of book

Moses life is divided into three sections of 40 years. He was 40 years old when he killed an Egyptian and fled to Midian. Afterward, Moses spent 40 years in the wilderness of Midian. During this time, he married Zipporah and tended to the sheep of his father-in-law Jethro, the Midianite priest. Moses later, speaks to God through a burning bush and receives orders to confront Pharaoh and lead his people out of slavery.

When the Israelites are set free, they spend 40 years wandering in the wilderness en route to the Promised Land. The Israelites ate manna that fell from heaven for 40 years until they were in sight of the Promised Land which was the border of the land of Canaan, Exodus 16:35. During their wilderness journey, Moses spent 40 days and 40 nights on Mount Horeb, the mountain of God; twice, Exodus 24:18 and Exodus 34:28.

The spies sent by Moses took 40 days to spy out Canaan; the Promised Land, Numbers 13:25.

It's recorded in Deuteronomy 9, Moses interceded on Israel behalf for 40 days and 40 nights because of the sins they had committed against the Lord. It explains that Moses laid prostrate before the Lord those 40 days and 40 nights because the Lord had said he would destroy Israel.

According to Deuteronomy 25:3, the maximum lashes a man could receive from his crime according to the Law was 40.

The Old Testament consists of twelve historical books. They are Joshua, Judges, Ruth, 1 Samuel, 2 Samuel, 1 Kings, 2 Kings, 1 Chronicles, 2 Chronicles, Ezra, Nehemiah, and Ester. They were written by different individuals, at various times and places. They have been arranged in a sequence that tells the biblical story of the Israelites entering Canaan, the rise and fall of the northern and southern kingdom, the returning and rebuilding of Jerusalem in the Persian era. The number 40 appears approximately 24 times in these Old Testament Historical Books. The majority are listed below.

Joshua was 40 years old when he was sent by Moses to explore and scout out the land of Canaan, along with 11 others, Joshua 14:7.

The land of Israel had rest, peace and was free from oppression for 40 years until Othniel the judge died, Judges 3:11.

Judges 5:31 is the last verse of Deborah and Barak's song. The Lord gave Israel victory over Jabin, the Canaanite king. The verse reads "So may all your enemies perish, Lord! But may all who love you be like the sun when it rises in its strength!" The people of the land had peace for 40 years after the victory.

Gideon saved Israel from the Midianites, and during his lifetime, the land had peace for 40 years, Judges 8:28.

According to Judges 12:14, Abdon had 40 sons and 30 grandsons, who rode on 70 donkeys. He judged and led Israel 8 years.

The Israelites did evil in the eyes of the Lord, again, so the Lord delivered them into the hands of the Philistines for 40 years. It was 40 years before God sent Samson to deliver them, Judges 13:1.

When Eli heard that the Philistines had captured the Ark of the Covenant of the Lord, he fell backward off his chair by the side of the gate. Eli broke his neck and he died, for he was an old man, and he was heavy. Eli led Israel 40 years, 1 Samuel 4:18.

Goliath came out for 40 days before being killed by a young shepherd boy named David with his slingshot. Goliath, the Philistine giant, measure over 9 feet and he wore a full armor came out 40 days, mocking and challenging Saul and his army to fight. Saul the King of Israel, and his whole army were terrified of Goliath, 1 Samuel 17:16.

Ish-Bosheth, son of Saul, was 40 years old when he became king over Israel, and he reigned for 2 years. The tribe of Judah remained loyal to David, 2 Samuel 2:10.

David was 30 years old when he became king, and he reigned 40 years, 2 Samuel 5:4. First Kings 2:11 explains that David reigned 40 years over Israel; 7 seven years in Hebron and 33 years in Jerusalem.

King David's son, Solomon reigned in Jerusalem over all Israel 40 years, 1 Kings 11:42.

According to 1 Kings 19:8, After Elijah ate and drank, he was strengthened by that food, and then he traveled 40 days and 40 nights until he reached Horeb, the mountain of God.

When Hazael went to meet Elisha, he took with him as a gift, 40 camel-loads with all the finest attire of Damascus. Hazael was sent by the king. He stood before Elijah, and said, "Ben-Hadad king of Aram has sent him to ask, will he recover from this illness?" 2 Kings 8:9.

In 2 Kings 12, Joash was 7 years old when he became king, and he reigned in Jerusalem 40 years. His mother's name was Zibiah, and she was from Beersheba. Joash repaired the Temple and did what was right in the eyes of the Lord, all the years Jehoiada the priest instructed him.

Nehemiah tells the people of Israel that each governor before him had been a burden to the people by making them pay for their food, wine and demanding 40 silver coins a day. Nehemiah makes it known to the people that he refused to accept the food that was allowed to him, Nehemiah 5:15.

The book of Psalms consists of 150 chapters, but only mention the number 40, once.

For 40 years I was angry with that generation;
I said, "They are a people whose hearts go astray,
and they have not known my ways."
Psalm 95:10 KJV

The Major Prophet books are Isaiah, Jeremiah, Ezekiel, Lamentation, and Daniel. There are only 6 verses which mention the number 40 in the KJV, and they are in the book of Ezekiel. A few verses are listed below.

The Ezekiel, the prophet laid on his right side for 40 days to symbolize Judah's sins. Ezekiel 4:6 reads, "And when thou hast accomplished them, lie again on thy right side, and thou shalt bear the iniquity of the house of Judah 40 days: I have appointed thee each day for a year."

Egypt laid desolate for 40 years because of God's judgment. Ezekiel 29:8-12 reads, I will make the land of Egypt desolate among devastated lands, and her cities will lie desolate 40 years among ruined cities. The foot of neither man nor beast will pass through it. And I will disperse the Egyptians among the nations and scatter them through the countries.

Ezekiel's temple is 40 cubits long. Ezekiel 41:2 reads, "And the breadth of the door was 10 cubits, and the sides of the door were 5 cubits on the one side, and 5 cubits on the other side: and he measured the length thereof, 40 cubits: and the breadth, 20 cubits."

Notes of Interests: A cubit is an ancient unit of measurement based on the forearm length from the middle fingertip to the bottom of the elbow. The typical length of a cubit is 20.24 inches for the ordinary cubit and 21.888 inches for the sacred one. So, 40 cubits would be about 60 feet.

~~~

Regarding the 12 Minor Prophet's Books, only Amos and Jonah mention the number 40. The book of Amos mentions it twice and it regarding the 40 years in the wilderness. The book of Jonah mentions it once and it regarding Jonah shouting to the crowds that 40 days from now, Nineveh will be destroyed, if they didn't repent. The people of Nineveh believed God's message and declared a fast from the king on down. The people repented, and God spared the city, Jonah 3:1-10.

The New Testament mentions the number 40 in the book of Matthew, Mark, Luke, Acts, 2 Corinthians, and Hebrews; a total of 16 times.

The number 40 is mentioned first in Matthew 4. "After Jesus was baptized, He was led by the Spirit into the wilderness to be tempted by the devil. And when He had fasted 40 days and 40 nights, he was afterward hungry," Matthew 4:1-2.

Mark 1 and Luke 4 also gives an account of Jesus in the wilderness being tempted by Satan during that time. Mark 1:13 reads, "And he was in the wilderness 40 days, being tempted by Satan; and was with the wild beasts, and angels ministered unto him." Luke 4:2 reads, "Being 40 days tempted of the devil. And in those days, he did eat nothing: and when they were ended, he afterward hungered".

In Matthew 24:12 and Mark 13:1-2, Jesus prophesied the destruction of Jerusalem, just days before his crucifixion. It was 40 years after his crucifixion, the Roman Empire destroyed the city and burned the temple to the ground in 30 AD.

After the resurrection of Jesus, he appeared to the disciples and a group of witnesses before He ascended to Heaven. It was 40 days between Jesus' resurrection and his ascension, Acts 1:3.

In the book Acts, the number 40 is mentioned in the following event. Peter and John miraculously heal a man who had been lame since birth. He was brought to the temple gate called Beautiful to beg from those going into the temple courts, Acts 3. According to Acts 4:22, the lame man was over 40 years old.

Notes of Interests: The book in the "Perfect Peace" series titled: <u>Isaiah 26:3-4 "Perfect Peace III" Silver and Gold</u>, published on 10/24/2012, speaks of this biblical event. Smile . . .

~~~

According to Acts 13:21, the Israelites requested a king, so God gave them Saul. He was the son of Kish from the tribe of Benjamin, and he served as their king for 40 years.

According to Acts 23:12-13, more than 40 Jewish leaders were involved in a plot to kill Paul. They had been exceedingly irritated and provoked by what Paul had said the day before in the council.

According to Acts 23:19-21, a young man told the commander what some Jews have decided to ask him to bring Paul down to their council meeting tomorrow to ask more question. They had plotted to have more than 40 men hiding and waiting to kill Paul. They have all promised not to eat or drink until they have killed him.

Other interesting information surrounding the number 40:

1. Jesus preached for 40 months.
2. The body of Jesus remained in the sepulchre 40 hours.
3. The 40 days of Lent starts before Easter.

4. The book of Exodus is the 2nd book of the Old Testament. It is the only book of the Bible with 40 chapters.

5. It generally takes 40 weeks for human pregnancy.

6. Forty is the only word of a number, where the letters all appear in alphabetical order; ex. F O R T Y = 6 15 18 20 25

7. The negative 40 degrees is the temperature where the Fahrenheit and Celsius scales correspond with one another, ex. -40*F = -40*C.

8. In American, 40 acres and a mule is an expression coined in 1865 when some freed slaves in America was given land and a mule to give them a good start in their new-found freedom.

9. In the Muslim religion, it is believed that Muhammad was 40 years old when he first received the revelation by the archangel Gabriel.

10. According to the Torah, the ritually impure are submerged in 40 measures of water, before they are ritually pure.

11. According to the Quran, a person is fully grown or mentally matured when they reach the age of 40.

12. WD-40 name come from the fact that it was the 40th attempt to create a penetrating oil and water-displacing substance.

CHAPTER 9

A Gentle Whisper

How does God speak?

The Bible says "After the earthquake came a fire, but the Lord was not in the fire. And after the fire came **a gentle whisper**. When Elijah heard it, he pulled his cloak over his face and went out and stood at the mouth of the mountain cave. Then a voice said to him, "what are you doing here, Elijah?" 1 Kings 19:12-13 NIV.

According to the Christian Book Sellers Association (2014), the top 8 Bible Translations are listed below. The phrase "a gentle whisper" is written as follow in those versions:

1. NIV reads, "came a gentle whisper."
2. KJV reads, "a still small voice."
3. NKJV reads, "a still small voice."
4. NLT reads, "the sound of a gentle whisper."
5. ESV reads, "the sound of a low whisper."
6. HCSB reads, "a soft whisper."
7. VOICE reads, "a quiet voice entered into Elijah's ears."
8. NASB reads, "a sound of a gentle blowing."

In other Bible Translations, the phrase "a gentle whisper" are listed below:

AMP reads, "the sound of a gentle blowing."
ASV reads, "a still small voice."
MSG reads, "a gentle and quiet whisper."
NET reads, "there was a soft whisper."
NLV reads, "a sound of a gentle blowing."
NRSV reads, "a sound of sheer silence."

The words gentle, gentleness, or gently means mild in temperament or behavior. The quality of being kind, or tender; not harsh or severe. According to 2 Samuel 18:5, King David commanded Joab, Abishai, and Ittai, "to be gentle with the young man Absalom for his sake." Absalom was the son of King David who held a revolt against his father. Absalom was the third son of David, his mother was Maachad, the daughter of Talmai, King of Geshur.

According to Job, his words were well received, because he spoke gently.

"After I had spoken, they spoke no more; my words fell gently on their ears," Job 29:22 NIV.

Gentle words have great power according to Proverbs 15:1, and Proverbs 25:15.

"A gentle answer deflects anger, but harsh words make tempers flare," Proverbs 15:1 NLT. "Through patience, a ruler can be persuaded, and a gentle tongue can break a bone," Proverbs 25:15 NIV.

Frequently, God speaks to us in a still and quiet voice that can be described as a gentle whisper or a soft voice. There are times when God's majesty is recognized when we are quiet. Psalm 46:10 reads, "Be still, and know that I am God. I will be honoured by every nation. I will be honoured throughout the world."

According to Isaiah 30:15, there is strength in quietness. "This is what the Sovereign Lord, the Holy One of Israel, says: Only in returning to me and resting in me will you be saved. In quietness and confidence is your strength. But you would have none of it."

Righteousness produces peace, quietness, and confidence. Isaiah 32:17-18 reads, "The fruit of righteousness will be peace; the effect of righteousness will be quietness and confidence forever."

The supreme example of gentleness is Israel's God. "He tends his flock like a shepherd: He gathers the lambs in his arms and carries them close to his heart: He gently leads those that have young," Isaiah 40:11 NIV.

In the Bible, "a gentle whisper" is only mentioned once. However, the word "gentle" is mentioned many times in the Bible in relations to various things, listed below are some of those verses.

1. Matthew 11:29, "for I am gentle and humble in heart, and you will find rest for your souls."
2. Matthew 21:5, "See, your king comes to you, gentle and riding on a donkey, and on a colt, the foal of a donkey."

3. Paul appeals to believers "by the humility and gentleness of Christ," 2 Corinthians 10:1.
4. The fruit of the Spirit is love, joy, peace, forbearance, kindness, goodness, faithfulness, gentleness, and self-control, Galatians 5:22-23.
5. According to 1 Timothy 3:2-7, one of the qualifications for an overseer is to be "not violent but gentle."
6. Paul wrote to Ephesians and urge them to live a life worthy of the calling they have received. They are to be completely humble and gentle, be patient, bearing with one another in love," Ephesians 4:1-2.

Now, the biblical event surrounding the prophet Elijah reveals, that the voice of the Lord can be a gentle whisper. Excitement can be great, and at times inspiration is good for us, but it is the whispers of God that bring clarity to our minds, direction to our lives and encourage us in His path for our lives.

First Kings 19:12 is the only verse where it is written that God is speaking in "a gentle whisper," and it was to Elijah. In brief, Elijah had just had a dramatic victory over the prophets of Baal on Mount Carmel. Elijah had the people to seize all of Baal's prophets and kill them, 1 Kings 18.

Queen Jezebel, the wife of Ahab the king of Israel was seeking to kill Elijah because all of Baals' prophets were killed under Elijah orders. Elijah ran into the wilderness until he came to a broom tree, sat down under it in despair, and fell asleep. God sent an angel twice with food and water to strengthen him. Elijah then travels 40 days and 40 nights until he arrived at Mount Horeb, and there he spent the night in a cave.

Shortly after, the Lord said to Elijah, "What are you doing here, Elijah?" Elijah told the Lord, he had been zealous for the Lord God Almighty, but the people of Israel have broken their covenant with him and torn down his altars. All his prophets have been killed, and he was the only one left, and they are trying to kill him, too.

The Lord then instructed Elijah to stand on the mountain in His presence. Then the Lord sent a mighty wind which broke the mountain rocks in pieces; then He sent an earthquake and then a fire, but His voice wasn't in none of them. After all that, Lord spoke to Elijah in "a gentle whisper." The voice said to Elijah, "What are you doing here, Elijah?"

Elijah was instructed to go back the way he came and go to the Desert of Damascus. He was to anoint Hazael, Jehu, and Elisha. The Lord told Elijah, he had preserved 7,000 others in Israel who had not bowed to Baal or kissed him! 1 Kings 19:9-18.

Because He is God, He is not confined to a single manner when it comes to communicating with His people. Listed below are other ways God had communicated.

1. Through a whirlwind, Job 38:1
2. By an earthquake, Exodus 19:18.
3. Spoke in a voice that sound like thunder, Job 37:2, and John 12:29.

4. God's voice is compared to thunder from the whirlwind, Psalm 77:18.

All through Scripture, the Lord spoke to and through His angels, prophets, and disciples. He also spoke to and through His Son, Jesus Christ.

In the past,
God spoke to our ancestors through the prophets
at many times and in various ways,
but in these last days he has spoken to us by his Son,
whom he appointed heir of all things,
and through whom also he made the universe.
Hebrews 1:1-2 NIV

The Lord speaks clearly to us through His Word. The more we read it, learn it, study it, and meditate on it; the more we will be able to recognize His voice, clearly and with certainty.

CHAPTER 10

Desert of Damascus

**The Lord said to him,
"Go back the way you came,
and go to the Desert of Damascus.
When you get there, anoint Hazael king over Aram."**
1 Kings 19:15 NIV

The oldest city on earth is believed by many scholars to be Damascus. It's one of the most ancient and well-known cities of Syria (Aram). In Bible days, Damascus was an important trade route. It had 3 major roads that led out the city. Damascus' western road led toward Egypt, its southern road led to Mecca, and the eastern road led to Babylon. Damascus was located approximately 133 miles northeast of Jerusalem. It had highly fertilized plains due to the river Barada. The river Barada is probably the "Abana" in Scripture.

Josephus, the Jewish historian says Damascus was founded by Uz, the son of Aram. Aram was the son of Shem, Shem was one of the three sons of Noah which makes Uz a great-grandson of Noah.

Question: Who are the other two sons of Noah named in Genesis 9:18?

1. H_____, the father of Canaan

2. J_____, he covered his father nakedness with Shem

Answer in the back of book

Damascus was a noted city in the days of Abram and is frequently mentioned in the Bible. It is first mentioned in Genesis 14:15, in connection with Abram victory over the confederate kings under Chedorlaomer. Damascus is the native place of Abram steward, Eliezer, Genesis 15:2. The city of Damascus is mentioned, next in 2 Samuel 8:5, when the Arameans of Damascus came to assistance Hadadezer king of Zobah. David struck down 22,000 of them because the Lord gave David victory over them in battle. In 2 Kings 14:28-29, before Jeroboam rested with his ancestors, he recovered Damascus and Hamath for Israel which had belonged to Judah.

In the reign of Solomon, Rezon fled from his master who was Hadadezer, king of Zobah. He became a leader of a band of men who revolted from Hadadezer, 1 Kings 11:23. Rezon the Syrian was also an enemy of King Solomon, 1 Kings. After Hadadezer's death, Rezon became king in Damascus. There was a long war between the Israelites and Syrians. At a later time, Syrian became Israel ally against Judah, 2 Kings 15:37.

The Syrians were subdued by the Assyrians. The city of Damascus was then taken and destroyed, and the inhabitants carried captive into Assyria, 2 Kings 16:7-9. The kingdom of Syria remains a province of Assyria until the capture of Nineveh by the Medes in 625 BC when it fell under the conquerors. After passing through various unpleasant circumstances, Syria was invaded by the Romans in 64 BC, and Damascus became the location of the central government of the province.

In 37 AD, Aretas the king of Arabia became the master of Damascus after defeating Herod Antipas. In 634 AD, Damascus was conquered by the growing Mohammedan power. In 1516 AD, Damascus fell under the dominion of the Turks; their present-day rulers. Damascus is the largest city in Asiatic Turkey, and Christianity exists within its walls.

According to 2 Kings 5:12 the rivers of Abana and Pharpar are rivers of Damascus. Naaman the Syrian who had leprosy dwelt in Damascus. The Prophet Elisha gave instructions through his servant Gehazi to tell Naaman to wash seven times in the river of Jordan in order to be cleansed of leprosy. Naaman made referred to the rivers of Abana and Pharpar in Damascus because those rivers were cleaner than the Jordan Rivers. Naaman was encouraged by his servant to wash in the Jordan River when he did he was cleansed of leprosy.

According to 2 Kings 8:7, Elisha went to Damascus, and King Benhadad the king of Syria was sick. He sent Hazael his servant with gifts to ask about his recovery. Elisha told Hazael to tell the king he would live, but the Lord had revealed in fact he would die. Elisha tells Hazel that the Lord had shown him that he would be king over Aram. He will severely destroy the Israelites because of their disobedience to the Lord.

In the New Testament era, Damascus contained Jewish inhabitants, Acts 2. Christianity made early converts there, the miraculous conversion of Paul occurred there. In Damascus, Paul was converted and preached the gospel, Acts 9:1-25.

In Damascus, a street called "Straight" is probably the one referred to in Acts 9:11. It is the principal street and runs for about a mile through the city of Damascus. This street is where Judas lived in whose house Saul was found by Ananias. Apostle Paul visited Damascus on his return from Arabia, Galatians 1:1-17. Christianity was planted here to preach the gospel which spread to the surrounding regions, Acts 9:20.

Damascus population is about 150,000 people and is considered one of the most beautiful cities in the East. The Orientals calls it "Paradise on Earth." The surrounding country is incredibly impressive. It is the purest city remaining compared to the other cities mentioned in the Bible. Damascus is known for its colorful woven cloth of silk and cotton.

CHAPTER 11

Anoint Hazael

The name "Hazael" is of Hebrew origin and it means "God Sees" or "God has Seen." The Lord sent Elijah the prophet to anoint Hazael to be king over Syria for the near future. Years later the Syrian King Benhadad became very ill.

Notes of Interests: Depending on the Bible translation the spelling of King Benhadad (KJV) is BenHadad, Ben-Hadad, Ben-hadad, or Ben Hadad. The name is also the name of 3 kings of Syria. The first Benhadad was the son of Tabrimmon, the son of Hezion, king of Syria who dwelt in Damascus. The kings of Syria had hostility toward Israel, but this King formed a league with Baasha, king of Israel around 909-866 BC. The second King Benhadad is regarded as the son of the first Benhadad. He ruled during the days of Israel King Ahab, Elisha, and Hazael; during 874-853 BC. The third King named Benhadad was the son of Hazael, the usurper. He was unrelated to the other two Benhadad.

~~~

Hazael is first mentioned by name in 1 Kings 19:15, and listed below is the verse in three Bible translations.

KJV: And the Lord said unto him, Go, return on thy way to the wilderness of Damascus: and when thou comest, anoint Hazael to be king over Syria:

NIV: The Lord said to him, "Go back the way you came, and go to the Desert of Damascus. When you get there, anoint Hazael king over Aram.

NLT: Then the Lord told him, "Go back the same way you came, and travel to the wilderness of Damascus. When you arrive there, anoint Hazael to be king of Aram.

The nation of Israel did that which was evil in the sight of the Lord. They became unfaithful to the Lord and served other gods. Their behavior caused the wrath of the Lord. The Syrian King Hazael became the Lord's instrument to discipline the Israelites for their disloyal and disobedient.

And the anger of the Lord was kindled against Israel,
and he delivered them into the hand
of Hazael king of Syria,
and into the hand of Benhadad the
son of Hazael, all their days.
2 Kings 13:3 KJV

Hazael was a 9th century BC king of Syrians. Hazael reign for approximately 37 years from 842-805 BC. He reigned longer than any other king and was very victorious during this era. It was under his reign that Syria the capital of Damascus became a mighty empire.

He also took control over large parts of Syria and the Land of Israel.

During those years, Hazael led the Syrians into battles against the troops of King Jehoram of Israel, and King Ahaziah of Judah. Hazael took control of the city Ramoth-Gilead, where King Ahab met his death during the fierce battle between Israel and Syria.

King Hazael oppressed Israel during the entire reign of King Jehoahaz. The Lord was gracious and merciful to the people of Israel and didn't completely destroy them. It was because of his covenant he made with their forefathers; Abraham, Isaac, and Jacob.

Jehoahaz prayed for the Lord's help, and the Lord heard his prayer. The Lord provided someone to deliver the Israelites from the hands of Syrians. Afterward, Israel lived in peace again as they had in former days, 2 Kings 12:4-5.

King Hazael died, and his son Benhadad became the next king. Then Jehoash son of Jehoahaz recaptured from Benhadad the towns that had been taken from Jehoash's father, Jehoahaz. Jehoash defeated Benhadad on three occasions, and he recovered the Israelite towns, 2 Kings 13:22-25.

Note of Interests: Hazael named his son after the king he killed; Benhadad.

~~~

The history of Hazael rise to the throne is given in length in 2 Kings, chapters 8-13 in the Bible. In brief,

Elisha is the prophet who succeed Elijah. He went to Damascus, the capital of Syria, and someone told King Benhadad, who was ill that the man of God was in Damascus.

Hazael was a high court official for King Benhadad before he became the Aramean Damascus (Syria) King who fought against Israel. His master, King Benhadad was very ill, and he sent Hazael to Elisha to ask would he recover from this illness. Hazael took Elisha 40 camels loaded down with the finest gifts of Damascus sent in honor of the king.

When Hazael arrived, he told Elisha, Benhadad king of Aram has sent him and wanted to know will he recover from his sickness. Elisha then told Hazael to tell the King he would surely recover, but the Lord had revealed to Elisha that he would in fact die.

Elisha begins to stare at Hazael until he felt ashamed and begins to weep. Hazael asked Elisha why he was weeping. Elisha told Hazael, he was weeping because he knows the evil that he will do to Israel. Israel strongholds he will set on fire, and their young men he will kill with the sword, and their little ones he will dash to pieces, and their women with child he will rip up, 2 Kings 8:11-12.

Hazael said, could a servant, who is a mere dog, accomplish such a great thing. Elisha answered, by saying, "The Lord has shown me that you will be king over Syria/ Aram." Hazael objected to the very thought of it but was assured that it was all part of the Lord's plans by Elisha.

Hazael departed from Elisha and went back to King Benhadad. He gave the king the message Elisha told him to give, that he would surely recover from his illness. Hazael returned the next day to see the king, and he took a blanket and soap it in water and place it over the king's face. As prophesized, Hazael seizes the throne due to the king's death.

King Hazael conquered several areas of the country east of the Jordan River, including all of Gilead, Gad, Reuben, and Manasseh. He captured the area from the town of Aroer by the Arnon Gorge to as far north as Gilead and Bashan, 2 Kings 10:33, thus accomplishing the prophecy of Elisha.

At the close of King Hazael life, he took Gath, 2 Kings 12:17. According to 2 Chronicles 24:24, he proceeded to attack Jerusalem and was about to attack the city when Joash bribed him, 2 Kings 12:18. Joash managed to obtained peace from King Hazael. He gave him all the gold that was found in the treasures of the house of the Lord, and in his palace, 2 Kings 12:18.

King Hazael reigned about 37 years and was succeeded on the throne by his son Benhadad, who on several occasions was defeated by Jehoash, the king of Israel. He was forced to restore all the land of Israel his father had taken.

It was approximately forty years later when Amos, in the opening of his prophecy, recalled Syrian battles against Israel. He also predicted the punishment that was to come upon Damascus.

This is what the Lord says:
"The people of Damascus have
sinned again and again,
and I will not let them go unpunished!
They beat down my people in Gilead as
grain is threshed with iron sledges.
So I will send down fire on King Hazael's palace,
and the fortresses of King Ben-
hadad will be destroyed.
Amos 1:3-4 NLT

~Remember~ Rest~ Rejoice~

CHAPTER 12

Anoint Jehu

Jehu was a military commander in the army of King Ahab, before being anointed king by the prophet, Elijah. He was the 10th king of the northern kingdom of Israel, 2 Kings 9:25. Jehu reigned lasted for 28 years. The biblical event of Jehu's life is written in 2 Kings, chapters 9 and 10.

Jehu was the son of Jehoshaphat. However, he is commonly mentioned as the son of his grandfather, Nimshi in the Bible. Nimshi is the father of Jehoshaphat, but don't confuse him with the other Jehoshaphat, who is the son of Asa, one of the kings of Judah.

Jehu name means "Jehovah is He." Jehu assignment given by God and presented to him by Elijah was to kill out the house of Ahab and wipe out the worship of Baal that had spread throughout Israel, at that time. Jehu was used by God to clean up the disorder and disarray, that King Ahab and Queen Jezebel had created in Israel.

According to 1 Kings 16:30, King Ahab did the most evil in the eyes of the Lord than any of the kings before him. King Ahab married Jezebel, the daughter of the king of the Sidonians. He allowed her idolatrous worship of Baal and Ashtoreth in Israel.

Question: Would this be a good time to reread Chapter 5; Jezebel?   Smile

God was patient for a while with Ahab and his many sins. Eventually, God's brought judgment upon his family bloodline, 1 Kings 21:20-22. Jehu is one of the three men who God chose to carry out His judgment upon Ahab's family. It started first with Ahab death. He was shot and killed in a battle against the Syrians by a random arrow, 1 Kings 22:34-38.

In brief, according to 1 Kings 19:15-17, God told Elijah to anoint Hazael to be the king over Aram, Jehu to be the king over Israel, and Elisha to succeed him as the prophet. Jehu would put to death any who escape the sword of Hazael, and Elisha would put to death anyone who escape the sword of Jehu." The bloodline of Ahab would be destroyed, by one person or the other.

After Jehu was anointed the king, he immediately took steps to secure the throne. Jehu knew that Joram, son of Ahab, had recently gone to Jezreel to recover from his wounds in a battle against the Syrians. Jehu hastened to Jezreel and killed two of Ahab's sons. He killed Joram, the king of northern Israel, and Ahaziah, the king of Judah, 2 Kings 9:14-29.

Notes of Interests: Joram, the 9th king of the northern kingdom of Israel name is also spelled "Jehoram." King Ahab and Jezebel, son. Don't confuse him with another man named Jehoram, who became the king of Judah. In fact, the Jehoram of Judah married Athaliah, the daughter of King Ahab and Jezebel.

~~~

The biblical event with more details is as follow. . . In the battle against Syrians at Ramoth-Gilead, Joram, the king of Israel was wounded. Ahaziah went with Joram to war against Hazael king of Syria. When Joram was wounded in battle, he left his army there to return to Jezreel to recover. Ahaziah, son of Jehoram king of Judah, went down to Jezreel to see Joram, 2 Kings 8:28-29.

In the meantime, Elisha had sent a prophet to Ramoth-Gilead to pour oil on Jehu's head. The prophet was instructed to tell Jehu that the Lord has appointed him to be king over Israel. Then the prophet was told to open the door and run away quickly.

The prophet, who name is not mentioned in scripture, sent by Elisha found the commanders of the army in council. He took Jehu from the council, and led him to a secret chamber, and there anointed him king over Israel. He told him he was to destroy the house of Ahab, his master, and avenge the blood of God's prophets, then the prophet flees immediately, 2 Kings 9:5-7.

When Jehu was asked by one of his fellow officers, was everything all right? Jehu informed them of what had been done and said. They immediately spread their cloaks and blew the trumpet and shout, Jehu is king! 2 Kings 9:11-14.

Jehu immediately with a chosen band set forth with all speed to Jezreel. There Jehu slew Jehoram by shooting him through the heart with an arrow, 2 Kings 9:24.

The king of Judah, Ahaziah tried to escape by fleeing up the road to Beth Haggan where he was wounded by one of Jehu's soldier in his chariot. He managed to escape to Megiddo where he died, 2 Kings 9:27-28.

Jehu then went to Jezreel, on entering the city, Jehu commanded the eunuchs of the royal palace to cast Jezebel out of a window. They threw her out of her window and her blood spattered against the wall, and the horses trampled on her mangled body, 2 Kings 9:30-33.

Jehu wrote two letters to Samaria. Jehu 2nd letter was addressed to the authorities in Samaria. He commanded them to appear before him on tomorrow with the heads of all the royal princes of Samaria. Seventy heads were piled up in two stacks at the entrance of the city gate. Then another 42 individuals connected with the house of Ahab were put to death, also, 2 Kings 10:1-14.

As Jehu rode toward Samaria, he met Jehonadab, a Baal worshipper. Jehu offered and gave him a ride in his chariot, and they entered Samaria together. Jehu then cunningly used Jehonadab to ensure that all Baal worshippers were in the temple to offer burnt offerings to Baal. Jehu had told Jehonadab, he wanted to have a great sacrifice for Baal and want all the worshippers in the temple. So, throughout Israel, it was proclaimed, and all Baal's worshippers came to worship him.

Jehu had 80 guards and officers in hidden, who was waiting to kill them all, 2 Kings 10:18-28. Jehu then burned the sacred stone and tore down the temple of Baal.

Jehu eliminated one idolatry, the worship of Baal, only to uphold another. He continues to allow the worship of the golden calves which was set up by Jeroboam in the cities of Bethel and Dan. The Lord blessed Jehu for his obedience. He granted him a dynasty that would last until his fourth generation because Jehu continued to hold to the idolatrous worship of King Jeroboam, 2 Kings 10:29-31.

Jehu, the 10th king of the northern Kingdom of Israel, reigned over Israel for 28 years. Jehoahaz, his son, succeeded him, 2 Kings 10:35-36. Jehu died a natural death during a time when the kingdom power and wealth were declining.

CHAPTER 13

Anoint Elisha

Elisha name means "God is Salvation." He was the son of Shaphat who was a wealthy land-owner of Abel-Meholah. Elisha became the attendant, disciple, and successor of Elijah the prophet. Elisha, the Hebrew prophet of the Northern Kingdom of Israel in the 9th century BC held the office of prophet for sixty years; 892-832 BC. It was during the reigns of Jehoram, Jehu, Jehoahaz, and Jehoash. He died during Jehoash reign. Elisha's period of ministry lasts much longer than Elijah. The life of Elisha is documented in the Book of Kings in the Old Testament, and he is only mentioned once in the New Testament; Luke 4:27 NIV and NLT.

"And there were many in Israel with leprosy in the time of Elisha, the prophet, yet not one of them was cleansed – only Naaman the Syrian."
Luke 4:27 NIV

According to 1 Kings 19, Elisha was one of the three men God told the prophet, Elijah, to anoint.

Question: Who are the other two men? If you don't remember the answer, start from

the beginning, reading this book again. . . .
and smile

1. _____

2. _____

Answer in the back of book

When Elijah found Elisha, he was plowing with 12 yokes of oxen which belong to his father. Twelve yokes of oxen equal a total of 24 oxen that indicates that Elisha's family was well-off. The prophet Elijah went over to him and threw his cloak over his shoulders and walked away. Elisha immediately accepted his calling. He left the oxen, ran after Elijah. Elisha asked Elijah to let him first say goodbye to his father and mother, and then he would follow him. Elijah says go. When Elisha returns to his oxen, he slew them, boiled and roast their flesh. He used the wood from the plows to build a fire to roast them with. Elisha then passed the meat to the people, and they all ate. Elisha then left with Elijah, and became his servant and ministered to him, 1 Kings 19:19-21.

Elisha was Elijah servant about 4 years before the death of King Ahab. He remained Elijah's close attendant for seven or eight years until Elijah was taken to heaven. During those years we hear nothing of Elisha except near the closing scenes of Elijah's life.

Notes of Interests: Elijah did not anoint Elisha with oil, but threw his cloak (NIV, NLT) over him. This a symbol of succession. Elisha has become the disciple of Elijah, but not yet his successor. The KJV reads, "and cast his mantle upon him." A mantle was a large outer-garment, probably made of sheepskin.

~~~

Beginning in 2 Kings 2, the detail events of Elisha's life emerges. Just before the Lord takes Elijah up to heaven in a whirlwind, Elijah and Elisha were on their way from Gilgal. Elijah told Elisha to stay there because he said the Lord had sent him to Bethel. Elisha told Elijah as surely as the Lord lives he would not leave him. While they were in Bethel, a group of prophets asked Elisha, did he know that the Lord will take his master away today, and Elisha responded, yes.

Elijah then asked Elisha to stay there because the Lord has sent him to Jericho. Elisha refused again, and so they go to Jericho together. The group of prophets at Jericho approached Elisha and asked him the same question that was asked of him in Bethel. Elisha gives the same answer.

Next Elijah tells Elisha to stay there at Jericho because the Lord has sent him to the Jordan River, and Elisha refuses to stay, again. So, they begin to walk on. Now fifty men from the sons of prophets went and stood at a distance, while Elijah and Elisha stood by the Jordan River. Elijah took his cloak, rolled it up and smote the river with it. The water divided and Elijah and Elisha walked across on dry ground.

Once across Elijah asked Elisha, what can he do for him before he is taken away from him? Elisha asked Elijah for a double portion of the prophetic spirit that energizes him. Elijah said it will be difficult but tells Elisha if he sees him when he is taken from him, his wish will be granted.

As Elijah and Elisha continue to walk together, suddenly a chariot of fire and horses appeared which separated the two of them. Elijah was then take up to heaven by a whirlwind. When Elisha saw the chariot coming for Elijah, he cried out, "My father, My father!" When Elisha saw Elijah no more, he rent his own clothes in two pieces.

Elijah's cloak fell to the ground, and Elisha picked it up and returned to the bank of the Jordan River. Elisha strikes the water with Elijah's cloak while saying "Where is the Lord, the God of Elijah?" Suddenly, the water divided into two parts for him, and Elisha crossed over to the other side.

After Elisha divided the Jordan River, the sons of the prophets said, "the spirit of Elijah rests on Elisha" and they bowed to the ground before him. The 50 prophets searched for Elijah three days but didn't find him. They thought that the Spirit of the Lord might have carried Elijah to one of the mountains or into one of the valleys.

The first miracle Elisha performed after he crossed over the Jordan River was in Jericho. The people of the city told Elisha, the water in the city of Jericho was bad, and the land was unproductive. Elisha told the people to bring him a new bowl and put some salt in it, and they did. Elisha then threw it into the water, and said, "the Lord has purified these waters. It will no longer cause death or make the land unproductive, 2 Kings 2:19-21.

Notes of Interests: Joshua had cursed the city of Jericho, Joshua 6:26. This is why the water was bad. After the Lord gave the city of Jericho into the hands of Joshua and the people of Israel. Joshua pronounced a curse on the city.

~~~

Afterward, Elisha went up to Bethel. While he was walking on the road, 42 lads started mocking his baldness. Elisha cursed them in the name of the Lord, and two female bears from the woods mauled them.

The book of 2nd Kings records the miracles that Elisha performed. His name is mentioned 49 times in 2nd Kings and 3 times in 1st Kings. Other interesting biblical events that surrounding Elisha are listed below. I pray you take time to read the events in its entirety; I believe you will be truly blessed.

The War between Israel and Moab 2 Kings 3:1-27
Elisha helps the Kings of Israel, Judah, and Edom defeat Moab.

The Widow's Oil 2 Kings 4:1-7.
Elisha multiplies and fills up jars of oil for a poor widow.

Elisha traveled to Shunem 2 Kings 4:8-17
Elisha blessed a barren elderly woman from Shunem to bear a son.

Child Sneezed Seven Times 2 Kings 4:18-37
Elisha resurrects the Shunammite woman's son.

Death is in the Pot 2 Kings 4:38-42
Elisha purifies poisoned stew.

20 Loaves of Bread 2 Kings 4:43-44
Elisha feeds 100 men by reproducing bread.

A Syrian General is Healed 2 Kings 5:1-19
Elisha heals Naaman's leprosy.
Gehazi Lied 2 Kings 5:20-27
Elisha servant, Gehazi is struck with leprosy.

Ax Head 2 Kings 6:1-7
Elisha makes an ax head float.

Elisha Defeats an Army 2 Kings 6:8-14
Elisha can hear miles away. Elisha had the ability to listen to the Syrian military officers conferring in Damascus over 100 miles away.

The Lord Opens the Servant's Eyes 2 Kings 6:15-23
Elisha blinds the Syria army.

Famine in Samaria 2 Kings 6:24- 2 Kings 7:1-20
Elisha prophesies a famine in Samaria.

Give Her Back Everything 2 Kings 8:1-6
Elisha helps the Shunammite woman again.

Elisha Meets Hazael 2 Kings 8:7-15
Elisha tells Hazael that he was going to be the king of Syria.

Jehu Becomes King 2 Kings 9:1-27
Elisha summoned a prophet to go travel to Ramoth Gilead
to find Jehu and anoint Jehu king over Israel.

Strike the Ground 2 Kings 13:14-19
Elisha's final prophecy to King Joash of Israel.

Moab Raiding Parties 2 Kings 13:20-21
Elisha's bones revive a dead man.

CHAPTER 14

Anoint

In Bible days, people were anointed with oil to signify God's blessing, protection, and empowerment.

The anointing was first instituted for the priests to be set apart for the Lord, and carry out the duties of the Temple. In Exodus 28:41, the Lord instructed Moses to anoint Aaron and his sons as holy priests who would minister unto Him.

Other individuals who were anointed were prophets, to boldly proclaim God's word, and kings to lead the people. Anointing was also mentioned in the Bible for healing the sick.

Anointing was the divinely appointed ceremony in the inauguration of kings, according to 1 Samuel 9:16 and 1 Kings 1:34-35. When a king or high priest were anointed, the oil would be poured over their entire head.

When an object was anointed, it was for a particular purpose, to be used as an instrument in the Lord's sanctuary. Anointing occurred for the consecrated of garments and vessels, also.

According to Exodus 30:32-33, the Jews were strictly forbidden from reproducing it for personal use. If anyone made it or put it on anyone other than a priest would be cut off from his people.

According to Exodus 30:23-24, the anointing oil was made from liquid myrrh, fragrant cinnamon, aromatic calamus, cassia and olive oil.

The New Testament Greek word for "anoint" is chrio. It means "to smear or rub with oil," and it signifies that an individual has been "consecrate for an office or a religious service."

CHAPTER 15

7,000

The study of individual numbers as they relate to the bible is called biblical numerology. The number 7,000 is mentioned 12 times in the NIV Bible. This number is believed to relate to "divine final judgment" by many scholars. It is mentioned ten verses in the Old Testament and two verses in the New Testament. My soul was truly enlightened by reading those verses, and they are listed below.

Old Testament
2 Samuel 8:1-13   David Defeated King Hadadezer
David captured a 1,000 of his chariots, 7,000 charioteers, and 20,000 foot-soldiers.

1 Kings 19:10-18   The Lord Appears to Elijah
Yet I reserve 7,000 in Israel, whose knees have not bowed down to Baal and whose mouths have not kissed him, 1 Kings 19:18.

1 Kings 20:13-22   Ahab's Victory Over Ben-Hadad
So, Ahab summoned the 232 junior officers under the provincial commanders. Then he assembled the rest of the Israelites; 7,000 in all, 1 Kings 20:15.

2 Kings 24:8-17   Jehoiachin Reign Over Judah

The king of Babylon also deported to Babylon the entire force of 7,000 fighting men, strong and fit for war, and a thousand skilled workers and artisans, 2 Kings 24:16.

1 Chronicles 18:1-13   David Conquers the Neighboring Nations
David captured a 1,000 of his chariots, 7,000 charioteers, and 20,000 foot-soldiers. He hamstrung all but a 100 of the chariot horses, 1 Chronicles 18:4.

1 Chronicles 19:1-19   David Defeats the Ammonites
They fled before Israel, and David killed 7,000 of their charioteers and forty thousand of their foot-soldier. He also killed Shophak, the commander of their army, 1 Chronicles 19:18.

1 Chronicles 29:1-9   Gifts for Building the Temple
Three thousand talents of gold (gold of Ophir) and 7,000 talents of refined silver, for the overlaying of the walls of the buildings, 1 Chronicles 29:4.

2 Chronicles 15:1-19   Asa's Religious Reforms
At that time, they sacrificed to the Lord 700 head of cattle and 7,000 sheep and goats from the plunder they had brought back, 2 Chronicles 15:11.

2 Chronicles 30:10-27   Celebration of Passover
Hezekiah king of Judah provided 1,000 bulls and 7,000 sheep and goats for the assembly, and the officials provided them with 1,000 bulls and 10,000 sheep and

goats. A great number of priests consecrated themselves, 2 Chronicles 30:24.

Job 1:1-5   Job's Wealth
And he owned 7,000 sheep, 3,000 camels, 500 yokes of oxen and 500 donkeys, and had a large number of servants. He was the greatest man among all the people of the East, Job 1:3.

New Testament
Romans 11:1-10   The Remnant of Israel
And what was God's answer to him? "I have reserved for myself 7,000 who have not bowed the knee to Baal," Romans 11:4.

Revelations 11:1-14   The Two Witnesses
At that very hour, there was a severe earthquake, and a tenth of the city collapsed. 7,000 people were killed in the earthquake, and the survivors were terrified and gave glory to the God of heaven, Revelations 11:13.

A Reader's Question

This new section just dropped in my spirit at 0613 on January 14, 2017, titled A Reader's Question.

An individual asked me the following question: "Why did I capitalize the word "Satan" on the Introduction page?

The Answer:

The main reason is that the three Bible translations, I research from the most has the word "Satan" capitalize, along with the other translations.

The word "Satan" is more than just a word; it's considered a proper name.

Author's Closing Remarks

In closing, I was truly blessed by writing this book. Basically, each chapter entwines with the other in some shape, form or fashion. I like that, it helped boost my memory, gave me clarity surrounding this particular biblical event and the individuals who were involved in it. I pray it did the same for you.

Among Elijah, King Ahab, Queen Jezebel, Hazael, Elisha, Jehu, Ahaziah, Joash, Saul (Apostle Paul), Gehazi, Naaman, Rezon, Abram, Ezekiel, Peter and John, Queen Athaliah, Obadiah, Joash and Jehoiada, Nehemiah, Joram, Noah, Moses, and King Benhadad which two captivated your mind, the most?

For me, it's Elijah and Elisha . . .

Elijah is known for great public miracles, while Elisha is recognized by the large number of miracles he performed. Elijah's ministry emphasized God's law, judgment, and punishment, while Elisha ministry greatly demonstrated God's grace, mercy, and loving-kindness. Elijah was like John the Baptist, preaching the message of repentance for sin, while Elisha was like Christ, doing miracles and deeds of kindness for individuals. Elijah came from a poor background, while Elisha came from a wealthy one; yet God used them both and in different ways.

Pray for the Ministry . . . May the "LORD of Peace," give you His Peace.

Dr. Vanessa

REFERENCES

Chapter 1   1ˢᵗ Kings
1.   Wikipedia, The Free Encyclopedia:
     https://en.wikipedia.org/wiki/Books_of_Kings

Chapter 2   1ˢᵗ Kings 19:1-18
1.   BibleGateway: https://www.biblegateway.com

Chapter 3   Elijah
1.   Wikipedia, The Free Encyclopedia: https://
     en.wikipedia.org/wiki/Elijah
2.   Jacksonville Theological Seminary
3.   Bible Study Tools: https://biblestudytools.com/
     dictionary/phoenicia-phoenicians

Chapter 4   Horeb
1.   Wikipedia, The Free Encyclopedia: https://
     en.wikipedia.org/wiki/Mount_Horeb
2.   BibleHub: biblehub.com/exodus/17-7.htm

Chapter 5   Jezebel
1.   Wikipedia, The Free Encyclopedia: https://
     en.wikipedia.org/wiki/Jezebel

Chapter 6   Broom Tree
1.   BibleGateway: https://www.biblegateway.com
2.   Biblehub: https://www.biblehub.
     com/1_kings/19-5.htm

Chapter 7   An Angel Touched Him
1.   Wikipedia, The Free Encyclopedia: https://www.
     en.wikipedia.org/wiki/Angel_of_the_Lord
2.   BibleGateway: https://www.biblegateway.com

Chapter 8   Forty Days and Forty Nights
1.   BibleGateway: https://www.biblegateway.com

Chapter 9   A Gentle Whisper
1.   BibleGateway: https://www.biblegateway.com/
     passage/?search=1+kings+19:11-13
2.   Biblehub: https://www.biblehub.
     com/1_kings/19-12.htm

Chapter 10   Desert of Damascus
1.   Wikipedia, The Free Encyclopedia: https://
     en.wikipedia.org/wiki/Damascus

Chapter 11   Anoint Hazael
1.   Wikipedia, The Free Encyclopedia: https://
     en.wikipedia.org/wiki/Hazael
2.   Jacksonville Theological Seminary

Chapter 12   Anoint Jehu
1.   Wikipedia, The Free Encyclopedia: https://
     en.wikipedia.org/wiki/Jehu
2.   Jacksonville Theological Seminary

Chapter 13   Anoint Elisha
1.   Wikipedia, The Free Encyclopedia: https://
     en.wikipedia.org/wiki/Elisha

2. Jacksonville Theological Seminary

Chapter 14   Anoint
1. Wikipedia, The Free Encyclopedia:

Chapter 15   7,000
1. BibleGateway: https://www.biblegateway.com

Answers & Information Section

Chapter 1
The Ark of the Covenant also known as the Ark of the Testimony is a gold-covered wooden acacia chest which contained two stone tablets of the Ten Commandments, Aaron's rod and a pot of manna.

Chapter 3
Elijah was told to anoint Hazael and Jehu. 1 Kings 19:15-16 KJV

It was by faith that Enoch was taken up to heaven without dying – "he disappeared because God took him." For before he was taken up, he was known as a person who pleased God. Hebrew 11:5 NLT

Chapter 5
The Church in Thyatira is the correct answer.

Chapter 8
What did God changes Jacob name to? God changed Jacob's name to Israel which means "wrestles with God," Genesis 32:22-32.

Chapter 10
The three sons of Noah are Shem, Japheth, and Ham. Shem, the eldest son of Noah, had 5 sons, and 26

nations came out of his descendants with several nations mentioned in parentheses.

1. Elam (Arabia)
2. Asshur (Assyria)
3. Lud (Lydians)
4. Aram (Aramaic, Armenia, Mesopotamia, Syria)
5. Arphaxad from which Abraham descended

Japheth had 7 sons, and 14 nations came out of his descendants with several nations mentioned in parentheses.

1. Javan (Greece, Romans, Romance—French, Italians, Spanish, Portuguese)
2. Magog (Russians, Scythians, Slavs, Bulgarians, Bohemians, Poles, Slovaks, Croatians)
3. Madai (Indians & Iranic: Medes, Persians, Afghans, Kurds)
4. Tubal (South of Black Sea)
5. Tiras (Thracians, Teutons, Germans, Scandinavian, Anglo-Saxon, Jutes)
6. Meshech (Russia)
7. Gomer (Celtic)

Ham, the youngest sons, had 4 sons and 30 nations came out of his descendants with several nations mentioned in parentheses.

1. Mizraim (Egypt)
2. Cush (Sudan, Ethiopia)
3. Put (Lybia)

4. Canaan (Hivites, Jebusites, Arvadites, Girgashites, Amorites, Arkites, Sinites, Hittites, Sidonians, Perizzites, Zemarites)

Chapter 13
The two men are Hazael and Jehu, 1 Kings 19:15-16.

Other Books by the Author:

Printed in the United States
By Bookmasters